MW01016756

Testi
Claudia Sugliano

Editorial coordination
Laura Accomazzo
Lara Giorcelli

Graphic design
Maria Cucchi

Translation
C.T.M., Milan

ISBN 13: 978-88-544-0299-7

2 3 4 5 6 11 10 09 08 07

Printed in China
Color separation: Grafotitoli
Bassoli, Sesto S.Giovanni
(MI)

CONTENTS

INTRODUCTION · PAGE 8

THE CAPITAL THAT ROSE FROM NOTHING:
THE HISTORY OF PETER'S CITY · PAGE 20

WHERE THE CITY WAS BUILT: THE FORT OF SAINTS
PETER AND PAUL AND VASILEVSKY ISLAND · PAGE 50

DOMES AND SPIRES FROM THE ADMIRALTY
TO THE PALACE SQUARE · PAGE 60

THE PRIDE OF THE CZARINA:
THE WINTER PALACE AND THE HERMITAGE · PAGE 68

LITERARY SCENES OF THE CENTER –
FROM NEVSKY PROSPEKT TO NEVSKY ABBEY
AND SMOLNY CONVENT · PAGE 88

SUMMER RESIDENCES:
PETERHOF: THE GLORY AND TRIUMPH · PAGE 108

CZARSKOYE SELO: THE PALACE OF
ALL THE RUSSIAS · PAGE 120

PAVLOVSK: BETWEEN NATURE AND REASON · PAGE 128

INDEX · PAGE 134

WHITE STAR PUBLISHERS

saint petersburg ❧

1 Immediately recognizable from the shape of the domes and its bright colors, the Cathedral of the Resurrection forms the heart of Smolny convent and is one of the best examples of Russian Baroque architecture. Begun by Rastrelli in 1748, the building was completed by Stasov almost a century later in accordance with the specifications left by the great Italian architect.

2-7 The vast extent of the hydrographic intersection on which St. Petersburg was built is clearly seen in this eighteenth century engraving. Wide, light-filled, spacious, and precisely laid out, right from the start the city was based on an architectural model that at the time had no equal among the disordered and crowded capitals of western Europe.

3-6 It is difficult to say which is the most representative work of Bartolomeo Rastrelli: the palace of Czarskoye Selo is certainly one of the most impressive in terms of size and for the successful application of the architect's unique Baroque canons. Under Catherine the Great, the interiors of the palace were redesigned by another master, the Scot Charles Cameron, in Neoclassical style.

INTRODUCTION

8 right Facing onto
the Neva on
Petrograd Island,
the Nachimov Naval
Academy, one of the
most important
scholastic institutes
in the city, makes
an elegant backdrop
to the Aurora.
The combination of
white and turquoise
and the stucco
decorations of the
1910-1912 building
were inspired by
the architectural
style of Petrine
Baroque.

8-9 Palace Square is
bounded on the south
side by the two semi-
circular sections of the
former General Staff
building, which are
connected to the
triumphal arch that
celebrates the victory
over Napoleon.
At 156 feet high, the
monolithic Alexander's
Column, raised by A.
Montferrand in honour
of emperor Alexander I,
is higher than Trajan's
Column in Rome and
the Egyptian obelisk in
Place Vendôme in Paris.

8 center left
The monument
dedicated to the
heroic "Defenders of
Leningrad" stands
in Victory Square.
157 feet high, the
obelisk stands in
a large enclosure
that symbolizes
the defeated siege.

8 bottom left
The cruiser Aurora
is famous for having
fired a salvo that
signaled the start
of the assault on the
Winter Palace. It has
been berthed where
the Great Neva meets
the Neva since 1948.

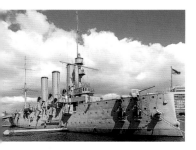

S t. Petersburg is an extraordi-
narily young city. What are its
three centuries of existence
compared to the millennia
that have shaped Rome,
Moscow, Venice, or Paris? Whereas
youth is a positive characteristic in the
life of human beings – whose brief existence must be lived to the full in their
early years – for cities it is generally the
opposite, as history has not yet had a
chance to weave its complex pattern.
St. Petersburg, however, is unusual
even in this sense. None of the city's
admiring visitors has ever got the impression of being in what until just "a
few" years ago was an inhospitable
northern waste-land, a desolate region
of Russia along the cold Baltic Sea.

The magnificence of Peter the
Great's creation on the outlet of the
river Neva in 1703 lies in the idea from
which it was born. The czar wanted a
new relationship with Europe. He
wanted to amaze both backward Russia and the civilizations he wished to
grow closer to. To do so, he dreamed
of an ideal city, a projection of Europe
"enlarged with the use of a magic
lantern on the luminous screen of
space and water" as Nobel prize-win-
ner Josef Brodsky wrote at the end of
the twentieth century, himself a citizen
of St. Petersburg.

The secret of St. Petersburg lies in
its European-style architecture – Classical, Baroque, Rococo, and Empire –
developed to suit the Old Continent
and here transported into an almost
metaphysical dimension by its vastness,
location, and color. Like pearls on a
necklace, the names of the European
architects can be strung together –
they were mainly Italian but also

French, Swiss, and German – that Peter the Great, then Elizabeth I,
Catherine II, and the other Russian
emperors invited to St. Petersburg,
the "Palmyra of the North." Soaked
in foreign culture, their inventions
merge with the surrounding environ-
ment to create a total work of art.
The European as opposed to Russian
design of the city – deliberately chosen to symbolize a break with the past
(the first example being the cathedral
of Saints Peter and Paul in Dutch
style anomalous in the Orthodox tradition of domed temples) – here has
many unusual features.

9 top left In the square of the Senate, the monument to Peter the Great seems to be crowned by the immense golden dome of St. Isaac's cathedral.

9 top right Palace Square has been the setting for important events such as Bloody Sunday and the October Revolution. It is dominated on the north side by the Winter Palace, the home of the Hermitage Museum.

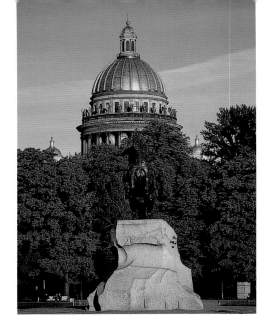

The city became the capital of Russia in 1713. The first Russian city to be built in stone and marble as opposed to wood, it challenged the fogs of the north and the immaculate whiteness of the snow with the colors of its buildings. The green of the Winter Palace, the red of the Beloselsky-Belozersky Palace and the fairy-tale church of Cesme, and the bright turquoise of Smolny Convent are typical of the "most premeditated city in the world" as Dostoyevsky defined it. Gold shines down from the spires and domes, almost taking the place of the rarely present sun. Horizontality is another aspect of this city-theatre, where Carlo Rossi created an imaginary link between the Triumphal Arch of the General Staff building, Palace Square, and Alexander's Column with the Baroque Hermitage, turning it all into a magnificent stage. This horizontality is then interrupted and directed vertically by the slender gold spires which, like electric signs, act as landmarks and break the monotony of the regularly square city layout.

St. Petersburg's appearance changes with the seasons and it is difficult to say when it is at its most beautiful. Autumn brings out the white Carrara marble statues against the multicolored backdrop of leaves in the Summer Garden. In winter, the snow covers the palaces with hoods similar to those worn by the Muscovite boyars who were so hated by Peter, and the ice, as if by magic, covers and sends the city's water "into hiber-nation." Late spring is announced by the melting of the Neva but the cold only really takes its leave, say the inhabitants, when the blocks of ice in Lake Ladoga float down to the sea. Summer, with its explosive blooms of lilies, brings the white nights when the sun only goes down for two hours each day and everything wrapped in a warm diaphanous sheen takes on a new dimension. Walking until morning in the miraculous night light, you feel you are a figure from a nineteenth century novel, for example, Dostoyevsky's *White Nights*.

Literature is another important page in the biography of St. Petersburg, which can be "read" in the works of great writers and poets like Alexander Pushkin, Nikolai Gogol, Fedor Dostoyevsky, Alexander Blok, Nikolai

12 top left The white of winter brings out the gold and turquoise of Czarskoye Selo, Catherine the Great's palace.

12 top right The statue of Nicholas I, here flanked by the elegant Hotel Astoria built by F. Lidval between 1911 and 1912, dominates St. Isaac Square.

12 bottom left The little Winter Canal is the narrowest and most charming waterway in the city.

Gumilev, Anna Akhmatova, and Josef Brodsky. The equestrian statue of Peter the Great in Decembrists' Square opposite the Neva is identified with Pushkin's *Bronze Horseman*. The busy Nevsky Prospekt – almost a metaphor for the city – cannot but be associated with the famous short story of the same name by Gogol. The characters from Dostoyevsky's works, forlorn and miserable, still seem to wander the streets and courtyards.

However short, the history of St. Petersburg has been intense and sometimes dramatic enough "to disrupt the world," with the October Revolution and the heroic resistance to the 900-day siege the Germans. The events in its history have marked the three changes in the city's name: the original, German inspired name, chosen by the xenophilous Peter the Great, was altered to Petrograd (its Russian version) during World War I for patriotic reasons, then in 1924 the city was almost inevitably renamed after the death of ideologist and leader of the Russian Revolution, Vladimir Lenin.

Whether St. Petersburg, Petrograd, or Leningrad, thanks to the love and commitment of its sovereigns, most of all Catherine the Great, and to the work of its Russian and European artists and architects, the city is still one of the most extraordinary and superb works of engineering and human genius.

12-13 *In spring, with the thaw, the Winter Palace is once again reflected in the Neva River.*

13 top *On the other hand, during the long winter, the Neva River covers with ice for a period ranging from 45 to 180 days.*

14-15 *The city of Peter the Great is the land of vast spaces, as this view of the palace's square demonstrates.*

16-17 *The statues of the spectacular Samson Fountain are reflected in the waters in front of the Great Palace of Peterhof, the summer residence built by Peter the Great on the Baltic Sea.*

18-19 *The immense holdings of the Hermitage Museum also boast the biggest collection in the world of Scythian-Greek jewelry, like the Solokha Comb dating back to the fifth to sixth century B.C.*

*21 bottom right
The new situation
created in the Baltic
after the brilliant
victory over the Swedes
at Poltava (1709) also
made possible the
transfer of the capital
from Moscow to the
young St. Petersburg.*

*20 bottom The
stubborn will of Czar
Peter I (1672-1725)
was responsible for the
founding of St.
Petersburg, portrayed
here by Jean-Marc
Nattier in 1717.
The sovereign was the
force behind the plan
to transform and
westernize old
Russia.*

*20-21 This painting
by Alexei Samsonev
shows a scene from
the establishment
of the first Russian
navy, created by
Peter the Great,
shown in the
foreground. The czar
had made a journey
to Europe in 1697
during which he
studied the
organization of
shipyards. Only the
revolt of the streltsy
at home prevented
him from visiting
Venice to observe
the construction
of the galleys.*

*21 bottom left
In this eighteenth
century engraving
by P.A. Novelli, Peter
the Great is looking
at the plan of the
Peter-Paul Fort on
the busy building site.
The fort was the first
nucleus of what was
to become the new,
splendid capital of
imperial Russia.*

When, in 1703, Czar Peter I gave the name St. Petersburg to the fort that he had built on the delta of the river Neva, he was already planning its future glory. The ruler of the great but backward Russia had chosen to turn his dream into reality on the boundary between the Baltic Sea and the Gulf of Finland in a land of marshes and mud where winter plunged the landscape into an endless night and summer was graced by an almost polar light.

Impetuous, yet rational and longsighted, this gigantic man who ascended the throne in 1689 at the age of seventeen after a childhood afflicted by bloody struggles for power, recognized no obstacles to his project. Disgusted by Asiatic Moscow and its intrigues, Peter dreamed of a flourishing and modern capital that would open a bridge to Europe. This bold idea was the result of Peter's experience in more advanced countries such as Austria, Spain, England, Holland, and France that he had traveled through on a long "study" trip in 1697-98. Neither the difficult geographical conditions nor the proximity to Russia's historical enemies – Sweden and Poland – discouraged him.

At the time, Russia was at war with the Swedes and armed clashes took place in the area in question; only the victorious battle of Poltava in 1709 and the Peace of Nystad in 1721 made life in St. Petersburg more tranquil. The uniqueness of the future capital of Russia lay in its origin. Rather than growing over millennia or even centuries, it rose from nothing due to the will of a single man, in a position that, though opening a window to Europe and providing Russia with an additional outlet to the sea, did not offer safe protection or ideal conditions to the port of the young Russian fleet, another of the sea-loving czar's creations.

Work began on construction of the fort dedicated to the czar's patron saints, Peter and Paul, on tiny Zayachy Island (Hare Island) in the summer of 1703. In order to follow the work personally, he installed himself not far away on the right bank of the river Neva in a small, four-room wooden house with a low ceiling. This was most likely a fairly uncomfortable arrangement for a man over six feet tall but one of his characteristics was simplicity and indifference to luxury.

Despite the marshy land, thanks to the physical labor of 20,000 men, the first fort was finished in a few months. Made from wood, which was an abundant material in the immense Russian forests, it was rebuilt in stone in 1706. The damp, unhealthy climate caused an epidemic of scurvy among the workers. To avoid halting the work, the czar assembled a mass of laborers brought from all over Russia (40,000 men), including common criminals. The strain and hardship was so terrible that St. Petersburg is said to be a city built on bones: almost 150,000 died in carrying out the enormous undertaking.

In 1704, the first of the great architects who were to design the city arrived from Denmark. He was Domenico Trezzini from Ticino in Switzerland. He was soon joined by Jean-Baptiste Leblond, a pupil of Le Nôtre, who was responsible for many of the bridges over the canals that cross the city and for the gardens of the royal palace which were inspired by those at Versailles. Peter I was also involved in the layout of St. Petersburg. His vision only allowed geometric regularity and may have been influenced by Christopher Wren's plans to rebuild London after the devastating fire of 1666. The center of St. Pe-

22 Nevsky Prospekt was cut through the forest between 1710 and 1720 and, right from the beginning, was the city's main street. Destined to become one of its symbols, it has been praised by poets and writers. In the foreground we see the Fontanka canal and the Anichkov bridge.

22-23 The city of St. Petersburg was built in the Neva delta where the river flows into Lake Ladoga. After a short stretch of 46 miles, it divides into a number of branches before reaching the Gulf of Finland.

tersburg was not based on concentric circles but on long, straight streets that intersect at right angles and a similar layout of the canals. The czar also laid down the standards for the design of the palaces along the roads and waterways, which were built in regular lines and initially inspired by the Dutch style. Midway through the second decade of the eighteenth century, Peter I decided to transform Vasilevsky Island (Basil Island) – the largest in the delta – into the city center with a network of canals similar to those in Amsterdam, but the plans drawn up by Trezzini and Leblond were never used.

St. Petersburg emerged from the waters on a forest of support piles that had been forcedly planted by an army of convicts under the threat of the

knut or whip. Some of Peter's other directives clearly indicate his iron will as a town planner. Not willing to spend any more than necessary, and in any case heavily committed in this enormous financial enterprise, he even ordered all future inhabitants to import one hundred rocks per year to contribute to the construction of the city. After the victory in the battle of Poltava over the Swedes, a wide road three kilometres long was traced out from the monastery of Alexander Nevsky (another of Trezzini's projects) that was to become the famous Nevsky Prospekt and the future heart of the residential city where the aristocracy's magnificent palaces were built. In 1713 an official decree from Peter the Great transferred the capital to St. Petersburg from Moscow, which had just been devastated by a fire. The decision met with great resistance. To overcome it, he offered a series of incentives and even "officially" transferred 12,000 Muscovite families to the city on the Neva! Wishing to stimulate the population's confidence in the network of canals that ran around St. Petersburg like a leitmotiv, the czar, crowned emperor in 1721, even prohibited bridges at first. A skilled sailor, Peter wanted his subjects to be sailors too, and in the large naval parades he was always present in the little boat he had learned to sail in as a boy.

"Ideologically" created as a European city, St. Petersburg was given its vitality by the work of engineers, architects, technicians, builders, and artists hired from various countries by the sovereign. When Peter I died unexpectedly in 1725 without leaving either a will or a successor, the new capital had already overtaken Moscow in size with a population of 75,000. Two years later, 90% of Russia's foreign commerce passed through its port. In fact, an edict by the czar in 1703 had proclaimed that the city had to be the port for all goods in transit from the Baltic or circulating in Russia.

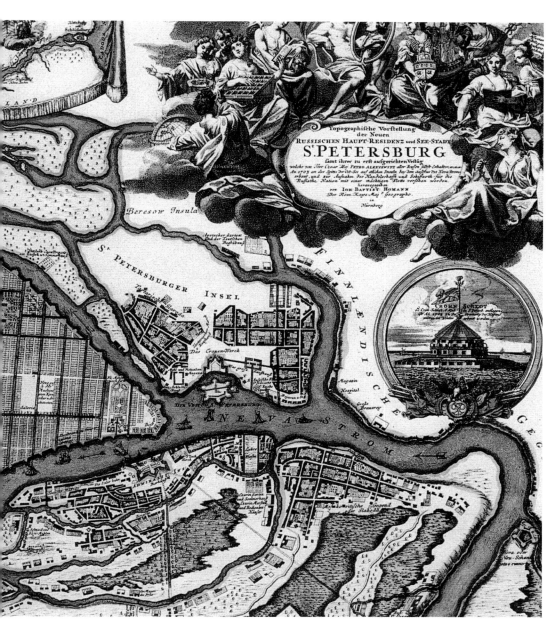

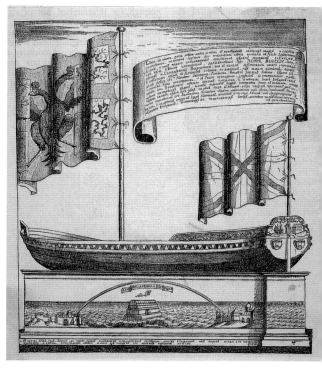

23 bottom Built at the request of Peter I in 1710, the Abbey dedicated to Alexander Nevsky, shown here in an eighteenth century view, was symbolically linked to the victory at Poltava. The monastic complex stands on the site where it was believed Alexander Yaroslavitch, the prince of Novgorod who was called Nevsky at the time, had defeated the Swedish army in 1240.

23 top right A Russian engraving shows the model of what was called "the great-grandfather of the Russian fleet." This was the tiny boat or, according to some, a Dutch lifeboat, in which Peter the Great had learned the art of sailing.

The death of Peter marked the start of a series of women sovereigns. Supported by the regiments of the Guard, Peter's wife, Catherine I, succeeded him but was to remain on the throne for only two years because of her excesses. On her death, the new czar was the twelve-year old Peter II, grandson of Peter I and son of the Alexis who had been assassinated in the fort of Saints Peter and Paul, accused of plotting against his father.

The young boy moved the capital back to Moscow where he died in 1730. St. Petersburg was restored as capital under the daughter of Ivan V, Anna Ivanovna (1730-1740), who was brought back from Courland, present day Latvia, where she had been living in poverty.

The new empress, whose reign has

24-25 This view of the Neva from the first half of the eighteenth century is unusual for the lack of bridges. The czar had prohibited their construction in order to force the inhabitants to use boats.

24 bottom left Educated in the west, Anna Ivanovna, the daughter of Ivan V (Peter I's weak and sickly brother and co-regent), brought the court to St. Petersburg and surrounded herself with German ministers.

been defined as one of the darkest periods of Russian history, transferred the center of the capital from near the Admiralty to the left bank of the Neva. It is significant that the three main arterial streets of the city – the Great Nevsky Prospekt, where in 1732 the coronation procession was held (the modern Nevsky Prospekt), the Middle Prospekt (Gorochovaya Street), and the Prospekt of the Ascension (that still bears the same name) – do not start from the royal palace but from the building that, at the time, was the czar's arsenal. Upon her death, the empress was succeded by Ivan, the young son of the empress' niece Anna Leopoldovna, who acted as his regent for 403 days, until Elizabeth, daughter of Peter the Great, burst into the palace at the head of the Regimental Guard and assumed power.

24 bottom right
Peter II, grandson of
Peter I, reigned from
1727 to 1730. These
years marked the
return of the court to
Moscow and the
exclusion from power
of one of Peter the
Great's best
collaborators and
friends, Prince
Menshikov.

25 bottom
The daughter of a
modest peasant
family in Swedish
Livonia, formerly a
chambermaid and
governess, Catherine
I, portrayed here as
empress by Jean-Marc
Nattier, succeeded
her husband Peter I
and reigned from
1725 to 1727.

27 top This work by an unknown painter from the second half of the eighteenth century shows the third Winter Palace designed by the Swiss architect, Domenico Trezzini. Today, these buildings have been replaced by the Hermitage Theatre.

27 center A lover of European culture, Elizabeth I (Peter I's daughter shown here in an engraving by E. Cemesov) ruled during the beginning of St. Petersburg's period of splendor.

With Elizabeth I (1741-1761) a period of splendor in the capital began and architectural work started up again in full swing. Elizabeth was a lover of luxury, entertainment, and beauty and employed the Italian architect, Bartolomeo Francesco Rastrelli, introduced a Russian version of the Baroque the best examples of which are the Winter Palace, the Smolny Convent, and nearby, the splendid summer residences of Peterhof and Czarskoye Selo. The Italian's work produced a successful and grandiose blend of western architecture with Russian elements. The figure of Rastrelli dominated the reign of Elizabeth uncontestedly. She was a woman of great appetites, a lover of European culture, and at the same time, of Russian traditions. During this period of

26-27 Plans for the magnificent summer palace, Czarskoye Selo, were drawn up by many architects before the empress Elizabeth I commissioned the building from the Italian architect, B.F. Rastrelli, in 1748.

26 bottom left and right Rastrelli's unique form of the Baroque can be seen in these views of the facade and plan of the Hermitage Pavilion at Czarskoye Selo.

transition, Russian society prepared itself for great changes. The "enlightened absolutism" that was to culminate during the reign of Catherine II began, magnificently reflected in the architecture and social and cultural life of St. Petersburg. It was in these years, that a poet defined St. Petersburg as "the Palmyra of the north," comparing it to the ancient Syrian city that had been a link between the West and East. This was exactly the role to which the Russian capital aspired.

27 bottom This painting by Pietro Antonio Rotari hangs in the Russian Museum. It portrays Bartolomeo Francesco Rastrelli, the favorite architect of Elizabeth I. He was the creator of masterpieces like the Winter Palace and Smolny Convent in St. Petersburg, the Great Palace at Peterhof, and Catherine's Palace at Czarskoye Selo.

However, Elizabeth died before she was able to move into the magnificent Winter Palace for which, Rastrelli had demolished all the pre-existent buildings on the site. The first sovereign to occupy the new palace was her nephew Peter III in 1761. He was an unhappy emperor, only half Russian, and educated in the spirit of Prussia by the generals of his father in the small principality of Holstein-Gottorp. By the end of the year, he had been ousted by his wife Catherine – a German princess who was born Sophie von Anhalt-Zerbst – during a palace plot led by Alexis Orlov, the brother of her favorite. Peter III was assassinated and his wife, instead of becoming regent to her son Paul, decided to reign alone over Russia as she had learned the language and been rebaptised Catherine in the Orthodox religion of the country. She was to remain in power for more than thirty years, from 1762 to 1796. Intelligent, astute, and filled with the spirit of the Enlightenment, the young empress wished to take Russia into the ranks of the great European powers and tried to continue the work of Peter I through internal reform and military conquests. Skillfully cultivating her image as that of an enlightened sovereign, Catherine II, attracted by the Encyclopedists, surrounded herself with figures like Voltaire, with whom she corresponded for fifteen years until the philosopher's death, and Diderot, whom she convinced to visit her in St. Petersburg. However Catherine did not put into practice the advice she received from the French philosophers and, instead, turned the peasant country of Russia

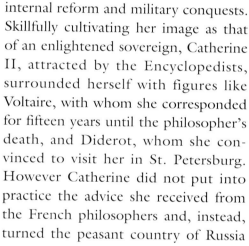

28 Catherine II continued the task of westernizing Russia begun by Peter I and took Russia into the ranks of the great European powers.

29 top right The proclamation of Catherine as Empress of all the Russias was accompanied by popular celebrations in the Palace Square in St. Petersburg.

29 center Peter III briefly succeeded Empress Elizabeth who died without leaving an heir. Feeble and sickly, in 1745 he married Sophia von Anhalt-Zerbst (the future Catherine II) who was the inspiration behind the plot to depose him.

29 bottom left Catherine the Great meets Diderot.

The advice of the great Enlightenment philosopher did not change the empress's policy that favored the nobility and their meeting in St. Petersburg at

Catherine's invitation turned out to be a disappointment.

29 bottom right This nineteenth century lithograph by De Lemercier shows an unusual image of Catherine II. Portrayed as an Amazon on horseback, the empress shows her strong-willed and independent personality that Diderot likened to a combination of the spirit of Brutus and the fascination of Cleopatra.

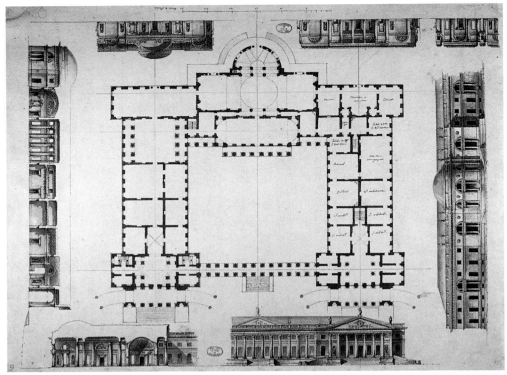

the epitaph "To Peter I from Catherine II" added to the emperor's famous bronze monument), she grandiosely continued the former emperor's work making St. Petersburg an imperial city. Her age was marked by the triumph of Classicism, which succeeded the Rococo and Rastrellian Baroque styles, and by her successful relationship with another Italian architect, Giacomo Quarenghi, who better than anyone was able to realize Catherine's conception of solemnity, greatness, and utility in architectural terms. In addition to the many wonderful aristocratic palaces in St. Petersburg designed by Quarenghi, there are also many public buildings. Among the unsurpassed works of the architect from Bergamo

30 Three engravings of Czarskoye Selo: top, plans for Alexander's Palace seen from the front; center, the Agate Pavilion, one of the park's loveliest buildings; and bottom, a detail of the Arabesque Room in the Great Palace. Alexander's Palace, built between 1792 and 1796, was designed by Quarenghi while the pavilion and room were the work of Charles Cameron.

into a state in which the nobility enjoyed all the privileges. In fact, during her reign, the number of serfs was increased by a million. Among her merits were, however, her great contribution to the development of education and culture in Russia (she founded, among other institutions, the Smolny Institute, the first scholastic institution for girls in the country) and her intense activity as a collector. She filled the Winter Palace with treasures reserved only for "her and the mice."

Believing herself to be Peter the Great's natural heir (she proudly had

are the Palladian style Hermitage Theater, the Smolny Institute (that stands next to the Smolny Convent designed by Rastrelli for Elizabeth), the Academy of Sciences, the English Peterhof Palace, and Alexander's Palace at Czarskoye Selo, with its magnificent colonnade.

Among the other foreign architects invited by the empress to St. Petersburg were the Frenchman Jean-Baptiste Vallin de La Mothe, the Scot Charles Cameron, the Russified German Georg Velten, and the Italian Antonio Rinaldi.

31 Created by the Italian architect, Giacomo Quarenghi (1744-1817), this pen and watercolor drawing illustrates the layout of the large park around Peterhof – the summer residence on the Gulf of Finland – and contains a sketch of the English Palace.

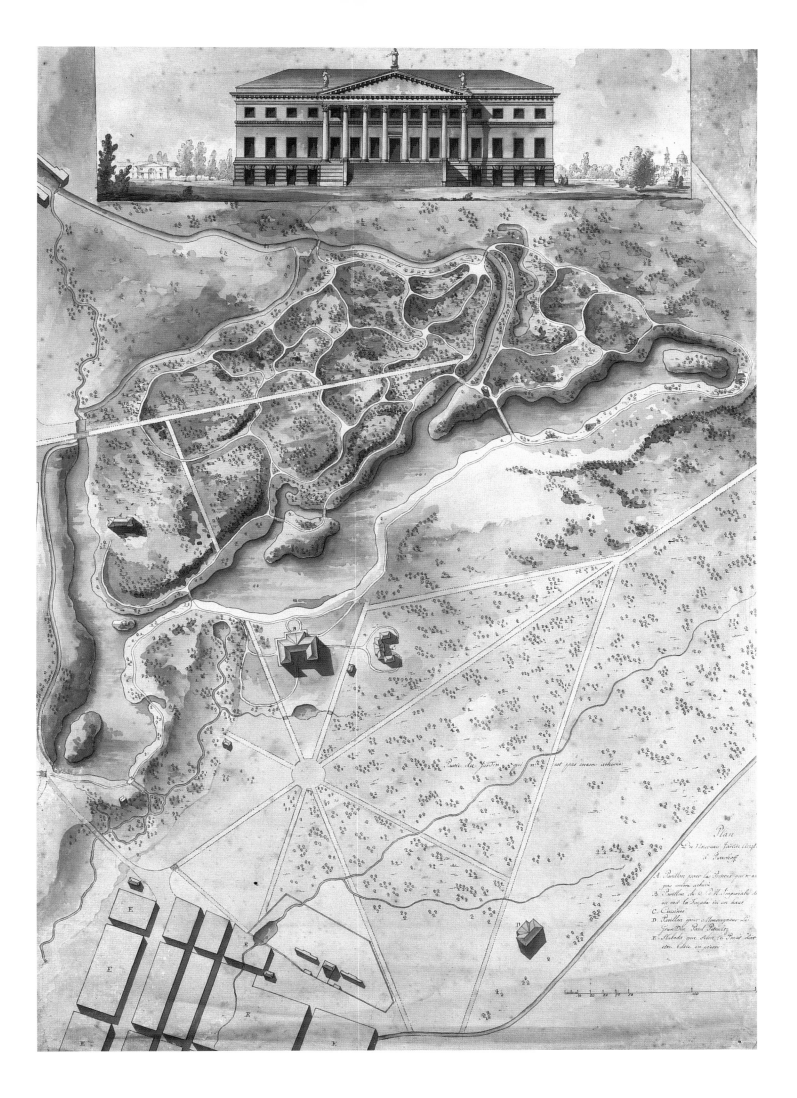

Plan
Du Nouveau Jardin Anglois
à Peterhoff

A. Pavillon pour les Princes qui n'a
pas encore achevé
B. Pavillon de S: de M: Imperiale dont
on voit la façade ici en haut
C. Cuisines
D. Pavillon pour Monseigneur Le
Grand Duc Paul Petrovit
E. Habods que selon le Projet doivent
être bâtis en pierres

Partie du Jardin qui n'est pas encore achevée

32 top Alexander I is portrayed in a classic equestrian pose in an engraving of the early nineteenth century. Next to him is a standard bearer holding the imperial banner with the two-headed eagle. The emperor ruled from 1801 to 1825 and was one of the protagonists of the Napoleonic Wars.

ALEXANDER, 1ST
Emperor of all the Russias, & the Imperial Standard.

32-33 This academic scene painted by Gioacchin-Giuseppe Serangeli illustrates the greeting of Napoleon I and Alexander I at Tilsit where, in 1807, peace between France and Russia was signed. In 1805, the Russian army had suffered a terrible defeat at the hands of the French at Austerlitz in which 11,000 soldiers died.

33 top left Paul I was assassinated in a bedroom in Michailovitch Castle. Built by the ruler to protect him from plots on his life, he only lived in this fort for 40 days before his dramatic death.

33 top right Alexander I, the son of Paul I and favorite grandson of Catherine the Great, was educated in the principles of the Enlightenment but ruled as an autocrat who gave little attention to the reforms that the new European power was in need of.

Catherine the Great's successor, her son Paul I (1796-1801), had been estranged from power and had almost always lived far from the court. He was hounded by the fear that his hated mother would have him suffer the same tragic fate as his father, making Paul I unstable and suspicious. As soon as he ascended the throne, Paul quickly distanced himself from Catherine's ideas and transferred himself from the Winter Palace to the gloomy Michailovitch Castle that had been designed by Vasily Bazhenov and Vincenzo Brenna. All his precautions, however, were to no avail and, on the night of March 12, 1801, the emperor was killed by conspirators in his bedroom. If the short interval of Paul's reign was not significant to the architectural history of St. Petersburg, that of his son and successor, Alexander I (1801-1825), Catherine's favorite grandchild, saw construction restart with renewed energy. The victorious outcome of the Russian campaign against Napoleon – definitively defeated in 1812 – was reflected in the building activity in the capital, designed to incarnate the country's newfound power.

33 bottom Emperor Alexander I (1777-1825) is shown here with his brother Constantine Pavlovitch (1779-1831), the viceroy of Poland. The magnificent granite-lined banks of the river Neva and the silhouette of the Peter-Paul cathedral in the fort of the same name form the setting of the scene.

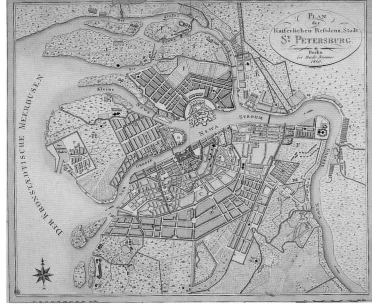

34 top left The Peter-Paul fort can be seen behind one of St. Petersburg's loveliest places through the arch of the gallery that crosses the Winter Canal to connect the Great Hermitage with the court Theater.

34 top right The equestrian monument dedicated to Peter the Great, celebrated by Alexander Pushkin, was built at the wishes of Catherine II to signify the continuity of her policies with those of the founder of St. Petersburg.

34-35 This view of the superb Great Theater is from 1812. The theater was built by Catherine II to replace an earlier wooden version. In its place today stands the St. Petersburg Conservatory and opposite it there is the famous Marinsky Theater, home of the Russian Ballet.

35 top Winter in St. Petersburg. Inhabitants move through the city on horse-drawn sleighs or on foot pulling their own sled. The frozen river was also used as a road.

The architects involved in this challenging new construction phase were the Russians Andrei Voronikhin (considered by many to be the founder of Empire style) and Vladimir Stasov, the Frenchman Thomas de Thomon, and the Italian Carlo Rossi. Like Catherine II before him, Alexander I was convinced that the politics of a State should be confirmed in the splendor of its cities. Of all of them, the style best suited to this concept was Empire style, developed in France and adopted in Russia in an even more solemn manner rich with sculptural decoration. In this period Palace Square was laid out, with the General Staff building that closes it on one side in a hemicycle, and the erection of the imposing granite Alexander Column in commemoration of the victory over Bonaparte. The Alexander Theater and offices of the major Russian state institutions – the Senate and Synod – were built during the same period. In St. Isaac's Square, the Frenchman Auguste Montferrand began the long, difficult construction of the square's cathedral, the largest in Russia.

35 center Prompted by Russia's new international role, St. Petersburg experienced a boom in construction around 1810.

35 bottom Vladimir Stasov (1824-1906), son of the architect Vasily Stasov, represented the typical St. Petersburg intellectual. He was a critic and historian of art and music, an archaeologist, and a scholar of philology and folklore.

The Great Patriotic War against Napoleon and the short stay of the Russian army in Europe had ushered in a wind carrying more liberal ideas that resulted in a number of young nobles forming secret societies that sought the installation of a constitutional monarchy in Russia.

In December 1825, shortly after the death of Alexander I and on the day of the swearing in of Nicholas I, a revolt, captained by young officers of the guard and supported by several regiments, broke out in the Senate square in front of the monument of Peter I.

The aim of the revolt was to make the senators sign the "manifesto of the Russian people" which demanded the end of the autocracy, the introduction of democratic freedoms, the abolition of serfdom, and the convocation of a Constitutional Assembly. The revolt was put down and ended with some officers being sentenced to death and the exile of many other of the Decembrists, as the rebels were called.

The reign of Nicholas I (1825-1855) was marked by the motto "Autocracy, Orthodoxy, and Nationalism," thus putting an end to all liberal aspirations and pushing Russia into a reactionary stage. The emperor's foreign policy was characterized by a stinging defeat in the Crimean War against Britain, France, Turkey, and the Kingdom of Sardinia. However, at home,

36 top The 1854 battle of Balaclava – this is the Charge of the Light Brigade – marked a heavy defeat for Russia in the Crimean War (1853-1856) fought against England, France, the Ottoman Empire, and the Kingdom of Sardinia.

36 center The final act in the Crimean War was the Congress of Paris which began in February 1856. Russia's representatives, Count Brunnow (a diplomat) and Prince Alexei Orlov, signed the peace treaty.

36 bottom The Decembrist revolt broke out in the Senate square on 14 December 1825 following the ascent to the throne of the reactionary Nicholas I. It concluded with the sentencing to death of several of the rebels and exile to Siberia of many others.

37 The frontispiece of the second volume by Schilder (1903) shows the czar with Grand Duke Michael and Alexander, the son who was to succeed him in ruling Russia. Alexander was to be known as "the Liberator" following his edict emancipating the serfs.

industry was introduced to the country which brought about the growth and transformation of St. Petersburg. Factories were built, the port was modernized and the city acquired the many-sided and contradictory appearance of the capitalist era. In 1837, the first railway line was opened, from St. Petersburg to Czarskoye Selo, the summer residence of the royal family.

Empire style was all the fashion but the "Russian Byzantine" style also appeared inspired by the Russified German, Konstantin Ton. The Marinsky palace on St. Isaac's Square and the Nikolaevsky palace were designed and built by Andrei Stakenschneider, another great architect active in the capital. He was responsible for inspiring the development of the Petrogradskaia storona district, a single artistic entity.

Alexander II (1855-1881) passed into history as the reforming and liberating czar as crucial changes in the history of Russia took place during his reign. Serfdom was abolished in 1861 and the following decade saw a series of administrative, financial, military, and scholastic reforms. Following acquisitions of territory in central Asia, the Caucasus, and the Far East, Alexander wanted to make his country more democratic. From an architectural point of view, the years of Alexander II were marked by the construction of large aristocratic palaces in Eclectic style, including the palace belonging to Grand Prince Vladimir Aleksandrovitch, designed by Rezanov. A terrorist's bomb brought an end to the life of Russia's most liberal ruler on March 13, 1881.

The atmosphere was stagnant during the reign of the reactionary Alexander III from 1881 to 1894 but St. Petersburg continued to develop. The new czar built the Church of the Resurrection in pseudo-Russian and Eclectic style on the site his father was assassinated. It was inspired by St. Basil's cathedral in Moscow.

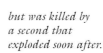

38 top The young Nicholas II was the last czar in the Romanov dynasty that had begun in 1613 with Michail Feodorovitch. The new emperor was weak in character and had little skill as a statesman. After

the death of his father, Alexander III, he inherited a country threatened by reactionaries and on the brink of economic collapse in spite of the rapid industrialization that had taken place in previous years.

38 bottom The bombardment of Rustciuk was an episode in the Russian-Turkish war. The engraving shows the Turkish redoubts and batteries and the Russian batteries.

38-39 Taken in 1881 in Copenhagen, this family photograph shows the emperor Alexander III (in the center holding a stick) and Grand Duke Nicholas (foreground, second left) who was to become the last czar of Russia.

39 bottom left On March 13, 1881, the terrorist group "Will of the People" ended Alexander II's life. The emperor had survived a first bomb attempt in the street that ran the length of Ekaterinsky canal

but was killed by a second that exploded soon after.

39 bottom right The funeral of Alexander III, who died in November 1894 in Livadia Palace in the Crimea. The funeral carriage wound through the city for four hours between two immense lines of people before reaching the cathedral of Peter and Paul where he was buried.

In 1894 Nicholas II took to the throne but he was destined to be the last emperor of the Romanov dynasty and the last emperor of Russia. His reign was marked by several difficult wars, like the one against Japan which ended in defeat for the Russian fleet at the island of Tsushima and the loss of Port Arthur in China. From 1890, after the industrial revolution in Russia, the country had to deal with a serious economic crisis due to excessive urban expansion and a difficult situation in the countryside where the peasants (85% of the population), though in theory free men, still depended on landowners. For St. Petersburg this was no longer a time

of prolific construction even if, at the start of the twentieth century, the new "modern" style (a Russian variant of the Scandinavian version of Art Nouveau) was used to embellish the city with fine-looking buildings, particularly private residences. The capital turned out to be the setting for the revolutionaries who, during the early twentieth century, brought down the czarist empire and founded the Soviet Union.

On January 9, 1905, 140,000 demonstrators, led by the Orthodox Pope Gapon, paraded in front of the Winter Palace bearing icons and religious standards. Nonetheless, the army fired on them resulting in the mas-

40-41 Nicholas II is accompanied by Alexandra of Hesse, the grand-daughter of Queen Victoria of England. The marriage between the two was held in St. Petersburg a few days after the death of Alexander III.

40 bottom
In December 1904, shortly before the end of the Russian-Japanese war, General Nogi and his General Staff were portrayed during an open air lunch.

41 top Nicholas II is seen at a parade with his young son Alexei, the long awaited male heir who was born in 1904.

41 center Food is distributed to the poor, including many children, in St. Petersburg during the reign of Nicholas II.

41 bottom The casus belli of the ill-fated war between Russia and Japan, Port Arthur was reannexed to Japan in 1905 after a long siege that ended in Russia's surrender.

sacre known as "Bloody Sunday." In Odessa during the summer of the same year, the famous mutiny on board the battleship Potemkin took place and, on October 17, Nicholas II, forced into a corner by the general industrial strike caused by dismissals at the large arms manufacturer Putilov, conceded the Constitution. The first Russian parliament, the Duma, met in April the following year in the throne room of the Winter Palace. Besides using force against the rebels, the Prime Minister, Stolypin, proposed an agrarian reform in 1906 that would create a new social class of independent landowners, the *kulaks*.

In 1914, the start of World War I caused the name of the capital to be changed to the patriotric and Russian style Petrograd, as a symbol of anti-German sentiment. Events moved quickly and the weak Nicholas II, easily influenced by the Czarina Alexandra, who in turn was influenced by the monk Rasputin, lost credibility in the eyes of his subjects. Nicholas was once more the head of an army that suffered serious defeats. The fourth Duma, which had remained faithful to him until 1915, eventually deserted him.

42 top Nicholas II and Alexandra Feodorovna are surrounded by their children in one of the loveliest and best-known portraits of the family of the last czar. From left to right, the Grand Duchesses Maria, Tatiana, Olga, and Anastasia, and, at the bottom, the czarevitch Alexei in a sailor suit.

42 bottom left Petr Stolypin, Prime Minister from 1906, instituted an agrarian reform that permitted peasants to own their land. Stolypin was assassinated in 1911 even though he had escaped death when his dacha was bombed in 1906 killing 32 people.

42-43 The rebel flag flies on the barricades during the 1905 revolution that began with strikes throughout the country. Russia's situation had worsened as a result of the disastrous war with Japan and "Bloody Sunday" when czarist troops fired on a parade of 140,000 peaceful demonstrators.

43 top A group of peddlers reads the czar's proclamation of the end of the war with Japan.

43 center left Rasputin is surrounded by several of his followers in his apartment in St. Petersburg. The empress was heavily influenced by him because his skills as a healer provided relief to the sick czarevitch.

43 bottom On the outbreak of World War I in 1914, the name of St. Petersburg was changed to the Russian Petrograd for patriotic reasons. Taken in August 1915, this photograph shows Nicholas II visiting the front with Count Dobrinsky, Grand Duke Nicholas and the head of the General Staff.

43 center right The mutiny on board the battleship Potemkin (part of the Black Sea fleet) while the ship was at anchor in the port of Odessa in 1905 turned out to be one of the first mass revolutionary episodes. Twenty years later, in 1925, the heroic action of the sailors was the subject of a famous silent film by Sergei Eisenstein.

An insurrection of workers and soldiers broke out spontaneously in Petrograd between February 23-27, 1917. Once *soviets* (councils) had been formed, the rebels took power in what was known as the February Revolution. In April 1917, Vladimir Lenin arrived at Finlandia station in an armored train. His speech marked the start of the second phase of the revolution and the ascent to power of the Bolsheviks, later to be known as the Communist Party. With the heart of the revolutionary movement based in Petrograd, the Smolny Institute housed the rebel's headquarters while the workers at the Putilov arms factory and the sailors in the Baltic fleet were the revolution's most effective supporters. The most important episode in the October Revolution took place on the night of October 24, 1917 with an attack on the Winter Palace in response to the bombardment of the counter-revolutionaries defences by the cruiser Aurora.

This event marked the grabbing of power by the Bolshevik Party and a turning point in the history of the city and all Russia. In 1918, the capital was definitively returned to Moscow and, on the death of Lenin in 1924, Petrograd was renamed Leningrad in his honor. The October Revolution was followed by civil war and a serious economic crisis. Private property was nationalized and thousands of workers were moved from the industrial suburbs to live in the large palace apartments in the city center during the 1920s.

Stalinist terror did not bypass the city. In 1925, vyev, the head of the party of the former capital, had criticised the NEP (New Economic Policy) which allowed concessions to the private sector. Partly for this reason, he was arrested and, in 1936, condemned to death. In 1934 Sergei Kirov had been appointed by Stalin as Secretary of the Communist party in Leningrad but, after eight years of power, perhaps because of his criticism of the dreadful living conditions of the workers, he was assassinated at the Smolny Institute which had become the party's headquarters. It was the era of purges. The first victims were Leningrad's intellectuals who were guilty of not following the directives of Zdanov, the ideological director of the Central Committee.

45 bottom left
The supporters of the Kerensky government await the attack of the revolutionaries in one of the rooms in the Winter Palace in November 1917.

45 bottom right
An endless line waits in front of a shop in Leningrad in 1931. The collectivization of agriculture instigated by Stalin – who came to power in 1924 – quickly led to a famine that killed ten million people between 1931 and 1932.

45 top Nicholas II and his children enjoy the sun on the roof of the conservatory at the Governor's House, their prison in Tobolsk.

45 center Two soldiers resting on a car have decorated their bayonets with the red flag. The photograph was taken in 1917 when the February Revolution forced the czar to abdicate.

45

One of the city's most dramatic episodes occurred during World War II during the 900-day siege of the city by the Germans from September 8, 1941 to January 27, 1944. With its three million inhabitants, the city remained trapped under German fire. On September 14, the Germans took Schlusselburg fort to the south-east of Lake Ladoga. Leningrad was then completely surrounded because the north was cut off by Finnish troops allied with Hitler occupying the Karelian isthmus.

Kronstadt naval base was also neutralized by air attacks but Hitler, though maintaining the artillery fire (the front lay 4 miles to the south-east), decided against a direct attack preferring to let the city fall because of the cold and hunger. The political heads of the city, which included Zdanov and Popkov, were confronted with insurmountable problems. Without an evacuation plan, the inhabitants, among whom were many hundreds of thousands of women, children, and old people, were trapped. Soon the daily ration of bread for the workers fell to 250 grams made with only 30% flour while the ration for everyone else was only 125 grams. The fall of Tivchin on November 9 cut the last railway communications to the east leaving Leningrad completely isolated. The only means of communication was across the ice of Lake Ladoga on which a "life line" 25 miles long was established to supply the city with bread. Other evils followed: the coal supply was exhausted and electricity was only made available for a few

46 top During the siege, which the inhabitants of Leningrad resisted with incredible heroism, the front line crossed Senate Square close to St. Isaac's cathedral. The great golden dome was repainted khaki so that it could not be used as a landmark for German air attacks.

46 bottom left The "road of life" crossed the frozen surface of Lake Ladoga in winter, as a result of which Leningrad was able to receive the supplies it needed to survive the siege.

46 bottom right The great palace at Peterhof, designed by Rastrelli, is nothing but a skeleton against a background of fountains – also destroyed – during the German occupation at the time of the siege. The photograph was taken shortly after the retreat of the German troops in 1944.

46-47 Nevsky Prospekt is under fire from Nazi artillery. Some flee but others were not so fortunate. In the 900-day siege, 670,000 people died, almost all civilians, partly from hunger and cold.

47 bottom During the terrible winter of 1941-42, Leningrad's water supply system froze up. Citizens were forced to get drinking water from the middle of the central Nevsky Prospekt.

hours each day. At the end of summer 1942, there were 750,000 inhabitants left in the city: 300,000 had died from hunger or cold, many were killed by the continual bombardments that struck mostly the destitute districts to the south-east of the city, and many more had been drafted or evacuated. On August 9, 1942, the day on which Hitler had decided his troops should enter the city in triumph, an exceptional event took place in the city. Dmitri Shostakovitch's seventh symphony was performed in the foyer of the Philharmonica and transmitted throughout the USSR and the world by radio. Life continued during the infernal siege and vegetables were planted in the Summer Garden and the

Field of Mars instead of flowers. In January 1943, after retaking Tichvin, the Red Army forced open the enemy block along Lake Ladoga where a railway, christened "Victory Road," was built. The siege ended on January 27, 1944 when the Germans were pushed back towards the west from the heights of Pulkovo. The exhausted city had to face reconstruction. At first this was limited to industrial buildings and architectural monuments, such as the summer residences like Peterhof which had been burned down by the retreating Germans. It was only later that buildings in Stalinist style were constructed outside the city center having no particular effect on the city skyline.

In 1948 terror returned once more with the so-called "Leningrad affair." Popkov, the head of the Communist Party, was shot along with other leaders accused of wanting to make the city on the Neva the capital of a federal Russia.

During the period from 1960 to 1980, Leningrad grew along the Gulf of Finland and in the areas to the north-west and the south. A large memorial was created in Victory Square which was dedicated to the heroes of the siege. With *perestroika* under Gorbachev at the end of the 1980s, another turning point was reached in the political and economic life of the city. Its mayor, Anatoli Sobcak, elected in 1990, was a charismatic and decisive figure. He opened the city to foreign investment and attempted to return it to the former glory that the repressive Communist

48 bottom left
In April 1996, while waiting to participate in a summit on nuclear safety, the President of the United States, Bill Clinton, leaves Piskarevskoye cemetery after placing a commemoration wreath.

48-49 Architects at work. In 1983, several members of the Research Institute in the Leningrad Project discuss work plans to build a residential zone on Vasilevsky Island.

48 bottom right
The Russian army in the post-Soviet era is facing a crisis but it seems that enthusiasm is not lacking. In 1999, a young man celebrated the anniversary of the parachute corps on a lamp-post in St. Petersburg.

era had obscured for so many years. In a clear indication of the road it wished to follow, a referendum in 1991 decided that the city would return to its old name of St. Petersburg and attempt to recover the noble traditions that had made it one of the most splendid and fascinating European capitals.

As it has entered the 21st century, St. Petersburg has become one of the most popular and prestigious cities in the world, attracting throngs of visitors. In 2003 it staged a lavish celebration to commemorate the 300th anniversary of its foundation. This marked a great tribute to the city created by Peter the Great, who would unquestionably be proud to see his magnificent capital rise to new splendor, admired the world over.

49 bottom left
The bronze horses that have adorned Anichkov bridge since 1850 were removed in summer 2000 for restoration. They had been removed only once before, in 1941, to save them from the bombardments.

49 bottom right
The city's modern shipyards are the fruit of Peter the Great's enthusiasm for sailing. Industrial infrastructure of this type has allowed St. Petersburg to make an important contribution to Russia's rebirth.

50 bottom John's Bridge, the oldest in the city built between 1738 and 1740, leads to the entrance of the Peter-Paul fort. The gate can be seen in the background.

50-51 Seen from the air, the star-shaped Peter-Paul fort is surrounded by walls with six bastions. Petrograd Island (referred to today as "the Petrograd side") is connected to the left bank of the Neva by Trinity Bridge. The large, horseshoe-shaped brick building used to be the Arsenal and is now the Artillery Museum.

Besides being the original nucleus of St. Petersburg, the fort of Saints Peter and Paul was a symbol of victory to Czar Peter I who, in 1700, had begun the War of the North against the Swedes for access to the Baltic Sea. At the time of its construction in May 1703, the river Neva was in the hands of the Russians. The fort was designed in the form of a hexagon and occupied all of small Zayachy Island (Hare Island). Up until 1740 it was known as "the city." After the brick reconstruction of the fort, designed by Trezzini, the solid walls (lined with blocks of granite between 1779 and 1785) surrounded a citadel containing the residence of the commander, the powder depository, the cathedral, the prison, and various other buildings. The fort was never used for defensive purposes (its cannon was used to announce midday from the times of Peter I and served to regulate clocks), but from 1712 on, operated as a notorious prison for opponents of the czarist regime. It housed many famous individuals, including the czarevitch Alexis (who died there, it seems, under torture), the writer Alexander Radiscev, Decembrist rebels, and Fedor Dostoyevsky, whose sentence of death was commuted in 1849 to four years of forced labor. In more recent times, the prison has housed Alexander Ulyanov (Lenin's brother who was sentenced to death) and the writer Maxim Gorky. Entrance to the fort from the east is through St. John's Gate, then down an avenue to St. Peter's Gate, the main entrance, built by Trezzini and still with its original eighteenth century appearance. It is decorated with symbolic figures such as statues of the goddess of war, Bellona, and of wisdom, Minerva, and the two-headed Romanov eagle. In telling the story of Simon Magus taken from the Acts of the Apostles, the low relief on the gable celebrates the victory over the Swedes in the War of the North.

Inside the fort, a stylised statue of Peter I enthroned, very different to traditional iconography, is the most unusual monument dedicated to the emperor. It was produced by the Russian sculptor Michail Kemiakin and donated to the city in 1991. The face of the statue is based on the wax mask made by Rastrelli for the famous wax figure in the Hermitage.

51 top left Designed by M. Kemiakin (1991), the monument to Peter the Great has already attracted a legend: whoever touches the czar's forefinger will have his wishes come true.

51 top right The site of Peter-Paul fort was chosen for its strategic position: it was protected to the south and west by the Neva and on the other sides by impassable marshes.

52 top left The interior of Peter-Paul cathedral, in which Trezzini skilfully united aspects of early Italian Baroque with northern Baroque, is richly decorated with frescoes and oil paintings. Pillars and columns in marble divide the interior into three naves. In 1870, the ceiling of the central nave was repainted with cherubim bearing attributes of martyrdom.

52 top right After Peter I was buried in Saints Peter-Paul cathedral in 1725, it became the burial place of the royal family. Of the 32 tombs in the building, only 2 are not covered by white Carrara marble lids, those of Alexander II and his wife Maria Alexandrovna, which are made from green jasper and pink rodonite.

52 center The building that holds the remains of the Grand Dukes was added to Saints Peter-Paul cathedral between 1896 and 1908 but now there is no room for more tombs. Designed by D. Grimm in Petrine Baroque style, the mausoleum matches the architectural context of the fort quite naturally.

Designed by Domenico Trezzini and built between 1712 and 1733, the cathedral of Saints Peter and Paul, the central monument of the architectural complex, has little in common with traditional Russian architecture, in which places of worship were cross-shaped, inscribed in a circle and topped by five domes. The cathedral, is more like a German or Dutch church for the length of its nave, almost like the main room in a palace with its large windows, and the high bell-tower (402 feet) with its gilded spire on which an angel holding a cross soars, one of the "vertical" symbols of St. Petersburg. The bell-tower was built first as it could double as a lookout tower in the event of war or, because Czar Peter loved the sound of the bells. The interior of the cathedral also deviates from tradition. Made luminous by its large windows, it has other elements unusual for a Russian church such as the pulpit and the large gilded iconostasis (1720). The latter, in the form of a triumphal arch — a suitable symbol to continue the theme of war and peace — is adorned with forty three icons and various statues, uncommon for an Orthodox church. The cathedral is also the pantheon of the Romanovs. The first to be buried here was its founder, in 1725, followed by all the other sovereigns and members of the dynasty until Alexander III, making a total of thirty two tombs. These are covered by white Carrara marble sarcophagi ornamented by a gilded cross, the deceased's name and, in the case of the czars, by four coats of arms of the Russian empire. Two funerary monuments differ from the others: that of Alexander II, the emperor assassinated by a terrorist, and that of his wife Maria Alexandrovna. The first is made from pink rodonite stone from the Altai moun-

tains. The other is in green jasper. The remains of the last emperor, Nicholas II, and members of his family lie in a separate chapel. They were shot on July 16, 1918 in Ekaterinburg.

52 bottom An attractive winter view of the fort from the river side. Behind the walls, which contain the Neva Gate and the commander's slipway, we see the complex of Saints Peter-Paul cathedral, the bell-tower with its slender gilded spire and, to the right, the dome of the Sepulchre of the Grand Dukes.

53 Saints Peter-Paul cathedral is the tallest building in St. Petersburg. Its spire is 402 feet high was originally made from wood and covered with copper. In 1720 it also became a clock-tower and was fitted with a Dutch carillon mechanism, the gift of Peter the Great, but it burned down and replaced in 1776.

МОНЕТНЫЙ ДВОР.

Right in front of the cathedral stands the small Boathouse built to hold the wooden boat on which Peter I learned to sail (now in the Navy War Museum). Other important buildings, all in early Petersburg Baroque, are the House of the Engineer and the House of the Fort Commander, which have been turned into exhibition rooms for the St. Petersburg History Museum, and the Mint, still functioning. It is possible to visit the former prison with its dark, gloomy cells in the Trubeckoi and Sotov bastions in the Alexeevsky lunettes.

The Neoclassical Neva Gate (1787) faces onto the river and opens towards the commander's slipway. It was also known as Death Gate because the condemned crossed it before being taken by boat to Slisselburg or Lissi Nos where they were put to death. From this point there is a dramatic view of the left bank of the Neva and the Palace embankment with a series of superb buildings: the Winter Palace, the Small Hermitage, the Great (or Old) Hermitage, the Hermitage Theater, the palaces of the Grand Duke Vladimir Alexandrovitch in Italian Renaissance and Eclectic styles, the palaces of Grand Duke Michael by Stakenschneider and, finally, the Neoclassical Marble Palace, an architectural masterpiece by Antonio Rinaldi given by Catherine II to her favorite, Grigori Orlov.

Vasilevsky Island (Basil Island) is the most important island in the delta (covering a surface area of over 27,000 acres). It was to be the center of Peter's city, according to the plans drawn up by Jean-Baptiste Leblond, with a long navigable canal and a grid of roads and smaller canals. The streets were called "lines" and each given a consecutive number, but, due to frequent flooding and blocks of ice which, during the spring thaw, isolated the island from the mainland, the czar's idea never came completely to pass. Thanks to its magnificent position and elegant buildings, the Strelka (Vasilevsky Island's easternmost point) which divides the river into two arms – the Great Neva and the Little Neva – remains one of the most attractive corners of the city. The most impressive palace – the old Bourse – was begun by Giacomo Quarenghi in 1783 under Catherine II and completed by Jean-François Thomas de Thomon in 1810. Built in Neoclassical style with a peristyle of forty-four Doric columns, it is inspired by the Temple of Poseidon at Paestum and is embellished with sculptural groups that symbolize domestic and foreign trade. Opposite the Bourse, today the home of the Central Navy War Museum, stand two red rostral columns 105 feet tall that were once the port's lighthouses. They are decorated with figureheads of ships, rostra and, on the bases, statues personifying the great Russian

rivers, the Volga, Dnieper, Volchov, and Neva. The section of Vasilevsky Island that faces the embankment of the University along the Great Neva is one of the loveliest places in St. Petersburg. It is home to a series of superb buildings such as a former Customs warehouse which now hosts the Zoology Museum with more than 100,000 items, including a giant mammoth found in the glaciers of Siberia in 1901 that lived more than 44,000 years ago. The second palace was built in Russian Baroque style and is crowned by a cupola and lantern. The pale green and white building is the Kunstkamera, which was Russia's first public museum. Built according to the wishes of Peter the Great, who was very keen on public education, the museum unites the collection of strange and curious objects that belonged to the sovereign with the collection that belonged to a Dutch anatomist, including human organs, limbs, embryos, and abnormal forms.

57 The Academy of Fine Arts is the last great palace on the University embankment and one of the most important examples of Russian architecture of the eighteenth century. The best view of the austere palace, adorned with copies of ancient sculptures of Hercules and Flora and watched over by two sphinxes, is from the other bank of the Neva.

It appears that the czar ordered that anyone who entered should be offered a glass of vodka and a roll of bread. A little to the south-west, the Academy of Sciences is an elegant Neoclassical construction (1783-1789) designed by Giacomo Quarenghi. The grandiose complex known as the "Twelve Colleges," (1722-1742), housed the offices of twelve ministries. It was commissioned from Domenico Trezzini by Peter the Great as a sequence of identical buildings in order to avoid disputes. In 1835, the ministerial pavilions, connected by an arched gallery, were ceded to the University where the famous chemist Dimitri Mendeleyev worked. Mendeleyev was responsible for the classification of the periodic table of atomic weights for chemical elements. The facade of the twelve colleges is the only one not to face onto the Neva because, it is said, the governor, Prince Alexander Menshikov did not want to sacrifice his vast French style garden. Behind the complex stands the palace that used to belong to this intimate friend and collaborator of Peter I. Designed by Mario Fontana and Gottfried Schaedel and finished in 1711, the two-story building with its mansard roof was more beautiful and sumptuous at the time than that of the czar. Infact, Peter preferred to organize receptions for foreign ambassadors and banquets to celebrate military victories there than anywhere else. When Menshikov fell into disgrace after the death of Peter, his mansion passed to the State and slowly

fell into disrepair. Now it has been restored and integrated with the Hermitage and is an unusual atmosphere-filled museum. It is an eighteenth century residence embellished with boiserie, Dutch stoves, rooms lined with tiles from Delft, and a large reception room built with oak. The adjacent Academy of Fine Arts was designed by Jean-Baptiste Vallin de La Mothe and Alexander Kokorinov and unites Baroque and Neoclassical elements on its facade, for example, the four-column loggias and the cupola on the pediment. Opposite, the Sphinx Pier takes its name from two mythical figures that stand on either side of the flight of steps that leads down to the river. The sculptures date from the reign of Amenhotep III and were found in Thebes in the first decades of the nineteenth century.

DOMES AND SPIRES FROM THE ADMIRALTY TO THE PALACE SQUARE

60 bottom The current appearance of the great Neoclassical complex of the Admiralty – the side of the building that faces the Neva is shown in the photograph – is the work of Andrei Zacharov who began its construction in 1806. It was intended to be a fortified shipyard when construction of the city was begun in the eighteenth century. Today, it houses the School of Naval Engineering.

The Admiralty on the left bank of the Neva represents the center of the city, and its tall gilded spire, visible from miles away, is a distinctive feature of the St. Petersburg skyline. The complex stands on the spot where Peter I built his first shipyard, protected by ramparts and moats, and where the first Russian warship was constructed. The current appearance of the Admiralty emerged between 1806 and 1823 when Paul I transformed the ramparts into avenues and Alexander I commissioned architect Andrei Zacharov to rebuild the complex. The result is one of Russia's most elegant Neoclassical buildings. Facing south, the main facade of the three-story palace is 1332 feet long and adorned with lions' heads and masks. The building's characteristic tower exceeds 236 feet in height and has an elegant colonnade. The elaborate sculptural decoration was dedicated to the foundation of the Russian fleet and the relief by Ivan Terebenev on the entrance arch shows Neptune handing his trident to Peter the Great. At the corners of the first parapet, we see the seated figures of Alexander the Great, Pyrrhus, Achilles, and Ajax, while the upper section of the tower – above the 28 columns – is decorated with statues that personify the elements, the seasons, and the winds. A gilded frigate that forms the weathervane on the top of the spire has been adopted as the symbol of St. Petersburg.

Of all the squares in St. Petersburg, Decembrists' Square – named after one of the most salient episodes in Russian history, the revolt of December 14, 1825 – is the site of what may be the city's best-loved monument, the "Bronze Horseman," immortalized by Russian literature when Alexander Pushkin wrote a poem about it. The statue was erected by Catherine II in honor of Peter the Great to symbolize his government. It stands in front of the western ramparts of the Admiralty and close to the church of St. Isaac where the empress got married. It was the philosopher Denis Diderot who suggested the name of the French sculptor Etienne Falconet, who worked on the project with his pupil Marie-Anne Collot (she made the head). The result is magnificent: the powerful sculptural image of Peter, wreathed with laurel like a Roman emperor, embraces the city with his gaze while his steed crushes a snake beneath its hoof

60-61 The dedication on the block of granite that forms the pedestal of the Bronze Horseman reads "To Peter I, from Catherine II." This laconic phrase was supposed to signal the continuity of the political work of the two monarchs.

61 top left
The Admiralty tower
with its high spire
topped by a frigate
dating from 1716
is the symbol of St.
Petersburg and has
become one of the best-
loved landmarks in
the city. It also marks
the center point of
St. Petersburg from
which the layout
of the city extends.

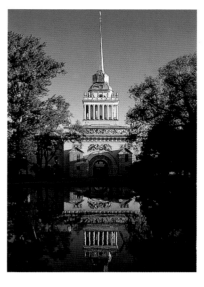

61 top right Angels
cross two standards
above the arch of the
central tower in the
Admiralty. The
sculptural decoration
of the complex that
commemorates the
naval power and the
victories of the
Russian fleet was the
work of Terebenev,
Schedrin, Pimenov,
Demut-Malinovsky,
and Anisimov.

as it climbs a rock shaped like a wave. The great emperor's left hand reins in the rampant horse, the symbol of Russia, and his right arm indicates the road to the North. The massive block of granite that forms the pedestal of the statue weighs 1600 tons; it was taken from a monolith and transported to St. Petersburg over a period of two years via the Karelian isthmus. After the defeat of Napoleon, Alexander I wanted to build the new headquarters of the Senate and the Holy Synod created by Peter the Great, on the west side of the square. The project was later brought to fruition by his brother Nicholas I. The twin buildings (1820-1834) are joined by a high arch adorned with sculptures and are the work of Carlo Rossi. They are the last examples of Empire style to be realized in St. Petersburg. The nearby Horse Guards Riding School, (1807), was designed by Giacomo Quarenghi in the form of a Greek temple and is adorned with statues of Castor and Pollux represented as horse tamers.

The vaults of St.
Isaac's cathedral
(left) were painted
by Fedor Bruni
(1800-1875), who
was one of the most
famous artists of the
age and head of the
Russian academic
school. The fresco
that measures 8783
square feet that
adorns the central
dome (right) was
the work of Karl
Bryullov between
1843 and 1845.

The other dominant construction in Decembrists' Square is the immense cathedral of St. Isaac, Peter the Great's patron saint, the first version of which was first built in wood in 1703 on the banks of the Neva. The Frenchman Auguste Montferrand won the competition to rebuild the cathedral following its destruction in a fire. Alexander I wanted it to be a magnificent construction but the water-soaked site created many problems and the construction was further slowed by continual alterations made to the design by Nicholas I. The project dragged on for forty years from 1818 to 1858. The building is a technical wonder as the foundations laid to support the cathedral's 300,000 tons were created by driving in 24,000 piles. The massive cathedral has an elaborate Corinthian portico on each of the four sides, supported by red granite columns roughly 56 feet high. There are large windows in the walls and the cathedral is crowned by four bell-towers and a high drum, ringed with columns, that supports the large gilded dome. Sculpture is a major feature of the external decoration, for example, the group of angels bearing torches by Ivan Vitali, that provides a link between the main volume of the building and its upper section. Equally remarkable are the high reliefs on the gables of the four pediments and the figures of the apostles and evangelists. The polychrome materials help to "lighten" the heavy structure of the cathedral: the grey granite of the walls, the red of the columns, the bronze statues, doors, and pediments, and the gold of the domes.

During the Soviet era, the interior was transformed into a museum (although still conserving that status, the cathedral is currently used for religious ceremonies on the most important Orthodox festivals). It is almost excessively elaborate but the skillful blend of different artistic media creates the impression of magnificence. Decoration of the cathedral required 1100 pounds of gold and 1000 tons of bronze, while the facings of the columns and altars used 16 tons of malachite excavated in the Ural mountains. Mosaics made using small tiles of this bright green stone give the impression that the columns of the iconostasis are monolithic. The icons on the first and second register on the iconostasis are made using a mosaic technique whereas those on the third register are painted. The fresco on the inside of the cupola, completed in 1847, is of *the Virgin in Glory* by Karl Bryullov and has a surface area of 8783 square feet. The extensive pictorial work on the walls and vaults of the building were the work of Fedor Bruni, one of the most respected artists of the time.

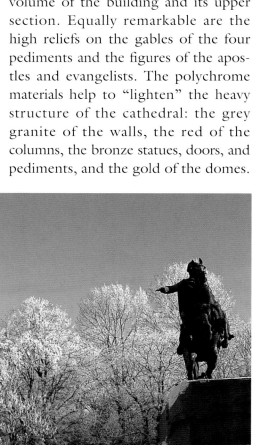

dome of St. Isaac's
cathedral is topped
by an octagonal
lantern and a
daring piece of
engineering
featuring three
overlapping shells.

square of the same
name, this view of
St. Isaac's recalls
Montferrand's
inspiration for the
cathedral: St. Peter's
in Rome and St.
Paul's in London.

65 center
The impression given by the St. Petersburg embankments is as much of well-ordered elegance as of freedom from monotony, even where the eighteenth and nineteenth century residences of the nobility beside the Neva give way to simpler, more "bourgeois" houses.

65 bottom An endless line of plain residential buildings is reflected in the Moyka. The river is less than 20 miles long but is one of the seven most important tributaries of the Neva. The marshy land on which the city stands is formed by morainic and alluvial deposits.

St. Isaac's Square was also designed by Montferrand and it was the Frenchman who produced the sketch of the majestic and ambitious equestrian monument of Nicholas I (it rests on the ground in only two points at the horse's rear hooves). The statue was then produced by Petr Klodt. The emperor wears the uniform of the Horse Guard – the most prestigious regiment – while the allegorical figures of Faith, Wisdom, Justice, and Power stand at the sides of the pedestal. Low reliefs illustrate important episodes in the emperor's reign, such as the quelling of the Decembrists' revolt and the inauguration of the St. Petersburg-Moscow railway line.

On the other side of the 328 foot wide Blue Bridge over the river Moyka (the bridge was originally painted that color), there stands Marinsky Palace, designed by Andrei Stakenschneider, which once belonged to Maria, the eldest daughter of Nicholas I. The elegant building housed the Provisional Government in 1917 and today contains the offices of the St. Petersburg City Council.

Also facing onto St. Isaac's Square, but with its entrance in Bolsaya Morskaya Street, is the historical Astoria-Angleterre Hotel, one of the most elegant in the city. It was designed in modern style (1910-1912) by Fedor Lidval and its name is linked to historical and literary individuals. It was from this hotel that the American journalist John Reed observed the Bolshevik seizure of power, which he was later to narrate in his book *Ten Days That Shook The World*, and that poet Sergei Esenin hung himself in his room in 1925.

Not far from St. Isaac's Square, the Moyka leads to a place of rare beauty, called Little Holland, a manmade island that was originally used to store wood during the reign of Peter the Great. It was named after Holland to commemorate the country where the czar had learned to sail. The architectural design of Little Holland was the work of Vallin de La Mothe, who produced a large and splendid archway framed on either side by Doric columns made from Tuscan granite.

64 The equestrian statue of Nicholas I (1859) in St. Isaac's Square was the last great work by Petr Klodt. It was by according to Klodt Montferrand's design. The enormous statue rests on only the two rear hooves of the horse. This complex technical solution invests the composition with great dynamism. The pedestal is decorated with low reliefs and allegorical statues.

65 top
The Neoclassical facade of Marinsky Palace, built between 1839 and 1844, – the first great work by A. Stakenschneider – dominates the other side of St. Isaac's Square behind the Blue Bridge. With its extraordinary original interior, today the palace is home to the offices of the City Council.

66 top left *This aerial view gives an idea of the magnificence of the Palace Square. The court on the right belongs to the Winter Palace which is connected by the Small Hermitage, with its hanging gardens, to the New Hermitage that overlooks Milionnaya Street. On the other side, the square is bounded by the marvelous semicircle of the General Staff building.*

66 top right *It is possible to see Alexander's Column and the Hermitage through the two monumental arches in the General Staff building, built across Bolsaya Morskaya Street. The attractive building was constructed by Carlo Rossi in 1819-1829 to house the Ministry of Foreign Affairs and the Treasury.*

66-67 *The 1968 foot facade of the General Staff building made it the longest building of the era. The design is enlivened by a superb arch that commemorates the Patriotic War of 1812. The decoration includes representations of the Russian army, flying angels, symbols of glory, and the chariot of Victory drawn by six horses.*

The course of the Admiralty comes out to the east in Palace Square, the most impressive square in St. Petersburg. Its architectural design combines the harmony and magnificence of the Baroque style of Bartolomeo Rastrelli with the Classicism of Carlo Rossi. The square is also imbued with the memories of crucial historical events. In 1905, it was the scene of "Bloody Sunday," when thousands of peaceful demonstrators found themselves under fire from czarist troops, and, on November 7, 1917, the culmination of moment in the Bolshevik revolution in the attack on the Winter Palace by Lenin's supporters.

On the side that faces the Neva, Palace Square is closed by the Winter Palace, originally designed in Baroque style by Rastrelli but rebuilt by Carlo Rossi in 1819. Rossi closed the south side with two hemicycles that are today the headquarters of the General Staff of the Army and the Finance and Foreign Affairs ministries. The two hemicycles are joined by a triumphal arch built to commemorate the defeat of Napoleon. The sculptural decoration by Stepan Pimenov and Vasily Demut-Malinovsky represents figures and arms symbolizing the glory of Russia, and an enormous chariot drawn by six horses above the arch is driven by the winged goddess of Victory. Certain rooms in the General Staff building – now part of the Hermitage Museum – conserve the original decoration by Carlo Rossi and an exhibition of Empire furniture and objects can be visited. Alexander's Column in the center of the square was raised in 1834 by Auguste Montferrand in honor of the czar who presided over the defeat of Napoleon. It is a monolith weighing 600 tons that, without supports, only maintains its balance thanks to its mass. The thick column is topped by a bronze angel bearing, it is said, the facial features of Alexander.

67 top *In Palace Square, one can often see the horse-drawn carriages tourists take to tour the city. This, the largest and most important square in St. Petersburg, has been the setting of dramatic historical events as well as always being a meeting place for the local inhabitants and an area for relaxation.*

67 bottom *Palace Square began to take shape in the mid-eighteenth century with the construction of the imperial palace. Almost one hundred years later, Carlo Rossi made his important contribution to its magnificent layout. The stylistic variety and harmony of its proportions make it an extraordinary monument.*

68 top left The elegance of the external decoration of the Winter Palace represents the swansong of Elizabethan Baroque. Despite its bulk, the palace is not cumbersome. Innumerable white columns seem to rise out of the ground to lighten the building, and the windows are adorned by lions' heads and terracotta colored cupids.

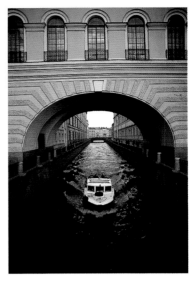

*68 top right
A gallery runs over
the small Winter
Canal that flows
into the Neva to
form an elegant
connection between
the Great Hermitage
and Catherine II's
court theatre,
designed by
Quarenghi. This is
one of the city's most
romantic spots,
rather like a Russian
version of the Bridge
of Sighs.*

*68-69 A forest of
vases and statues of
heroes and gods dear
to the hearts of the
city population lines
the balustrade on the
south face of the
Winter Palace. Built
as a winter residence
for the czarina
Elizabeth, the
building was partly
used as a hospital
during World War I
and became the seat
of the government in
1917.*

THE PRIDE OF THE CZARINA: THE WINTER PALACE AND THE HERMITAGE

*69 bottom
The principal facade
of the New
Hermitage overlooks
Millionnaya Street.
It was built between
1839 and 1851 to
accommodate the
increasing number
of works of art held
in the older building,
Russia's first real
museum. Ten
powerful Atlantes
carved from single
pieces of granite by
A. Terebenev support
the portico that used
to be the entrance
to the museum.
In 1852, Nicholas I
opened the museum
to the public for the
first time.*

The Winter Palace is the former residence of the Russian imperial family and today houses the Hermitage Museum. It is the most famous and most extraordinary building in the square that proudly rivals Red Square in Moscow. At the time of Anna Ivanovna's reign (1730-1740), the area was still wild enough for a ban to be necessary on the shooting of hares and, during the early years of Elizabeth I's reign (1742-1761), oats were still grown there. However, it was under Elizabeth that construction of the Winter Palace began and the area was transformed into an enormous construction site. The plan of Peter the Great's daughter (who was as committed as her father to making Russia's new capital magnificent) to build in this spot was not the first. More or less in the same area along the banks of the Neva and close to the Admiralty, three other buildings had previously been con-

structed: Peter's modest, two-story house (1711), his slightly larger residence with a Dutch-style pointed roof in which he was to die in 1725, and an elegant palace designed by Domenico Trezzini. Initially it was Bartolomeo Rastrelli (court architect from 1736 and Elizabeth I's preferred architect who strongly influenced the city's Baroque image) that rebuilt and expanded the last building but, in 1754, he was asked to build a completely new one. To do so, Rastrelli drew up an elaborate project that required the demolition of the existing buildings and a ban on the use of both wood and stone in the area of the rivers and Lake Ladoga for three years, these being materials reserved for construction of the Winter Palace. The work required 2000 men and produced what can be described as the swan song of "Elizabethan" Russian Baroque style. In a dramatic contrast with the simple rectangular plan of the grandiose building, Rastrelli created external and internal decoration of unique imagination and elegance. The enormous palace had over 1000 rooms and was neither uniform nor monotonous. The multitude of white columns resemble plant stems that grow out of the ground. They are gathered in bunches at the corners but thin out elsewhere to allow space for the 2000 white-framed windows adorned with lions' heads and terracotta-colored cherubim. The originality of the design is emphasized by the painted walls

70 The copy of a Roman mosaic decorates the floor of the nineteenth century Pavilion Room. Reproductions of the Fountain of Tears, from Bachcisarai Palace in the Crimea, stand among the elegant white columns.

whose color has been altered on several occasions. For instance, at the start of the twentieth century they were purplish red, later pale pink, and today they are green. The balustrade on the roof provides the base for a forest of vases and statues of heroes and divinities that are dear to the mythology of St. Petersburg. From here, the view of the city with its golden domes and spires is enchanting.

Rastrelli's superb interiors were almost all lost in the terrible fire of 1837, with the exception of the Ambassadors' (or Jordan) Stairway. On January 6, the day of the Epiphany, the czar and his retinue were going down the stairs on their way to banks of the Neva where the waters were to be blessed in commemoration of the baptism of Christ. In this high luminous space, white with golden friezes, the light enters in shafts from the windows and is reflected in the mirrors onto the statues of gods and muses. Elizabeth died before seeing her palace completed so that, in 1762, it was Catherine II who took possession of the Winter Palace. The purchase of the picture collection of the Berlin dealer Gotzkowsky in 1764 – 225 works by Dutch and Flemish masters – marked the origin of the future Hermitage Museum. The sovereign's passion for collecting (realizing the political and personal prestige she would acquire from it) ensured that the nucleus of the museum's collection grew at a dizzying rate. In 1768, she added 600 works and, four years later, 400 canvases from the Crozat collection, the most famous collection of the eighteenth century, including *Judith* by Giorgione, and *Danae* and the *Nativity* by Rembrandt. At that point, the empress decided to enlarge the Winter Palace which led to the construction of the Small Hermitage between 1764 and 1775, designed by Jean-Baptiste

71 top left A lovely nineteenth century stone vase adorns the Malachite Room which was once the drawing room of the apartment that belonged to Nicholas I's consort. Designed by A. Bryullov, the room has eight columns, eight pillars, and two fireplaces carved from the lovely green stone from the Urals. The decoration is based on the Russian mosaic technique.

71 top right The Hermitage's collections include many superb French and Flemish tapestries. The refined aesthetic tastes of the emperors created the nucleus of what has become one of the most important museums in the world. Even during the difficult years that followed the revolution, the Hermitage continued to acquire outstanding works of art.

72 The large Italian room known as the "skylights Room," designed by the German architect, Leo von Klenze for Nicholas I, is in the New Hermitage and is open to the public as a museum. The walls are hung with paintings by the Italian school but there are also works of art such as the large vases made from semi-precious stone from the Urals.

73 top left The Hermitage's collection of Flemish art is one of the most impressive in the museum. The photograph shows Portrait of a Family by Van Dyck (1599-1641) and is one of the most beautiful by the artist in the palace. Others by Van Dyck include a series of official portraits and a romantic self-portrait.

During the reign of Catherine's son, Paul I, the palace ceased to be solely the location of the imperial private collection but it was not until the reign of Alexander I – following the fall of Napoleon the great European collections were opened to the public – that the idea of allowing visitors to view it was first considered.

Later, Nicholas I had Vasily Stasov rebuild the Winter Palace in just two years after it was burned down in 1837 (all the works of art were saved,

73 bottom left Designed by Quarenghi in the 1780's, this gallery is a copy of Raphaello's Loggias in the Vatican Museum. The frescoes on the walls and ceiling were copied in tempera on pieces of canvas and sent to St. Petersburg for Catherine II.

73 bottom right Beyond the room that precedes Raphaello's Loggias, embellished with grotesque wall decorations and parquet flooring, stretches the long, magnificent gallery.

Vallin de La Mothe. Catherine's library was arranged in two galleries of the building on the Neva, embellished by a hanging garden in the center, then transferred to a suite of rooms in the palace referred to as the Old Hermitage built by Yuri Felyten between 1771 and 1787. Another Italian architect, Giacomo Quarenghi, designed the Theater in that period, which was joined to the Old Hermitage by a gallery that ran above the Small Winter Canal, closely resembling a view of Venice. Inspired by Palladian architecture, the theatre was informal in style. Guests were allowed to sit anywhere on the simple wooden benches. Members of the imperial family often took part in performances and concerts were conducted by famous composers like Paisiello and Cimarosa. Quarenghi was also responsible for Raphaello's Loggias, which were a reproduction on Russian soil of the rooms decorated by the master in the Vatican.

73 centre left Peter I's Small Throne Room was built in 1833 by Montferrand and rebuilt by Stasov after the 1837 fire.

Inside the enormous niche – framed by white marble columns with gilt bases and capitals – there is the large painting of Minerva and Peter by J. Amiconi. The oak and gilded silver imperial throne is a wonderful example of English cabinet-making.

74 *The large Coats of Arms' Room measures over 10,000 square feet in area and was decorated by V. Stasov. The originality of the room comes from the double Corinthian columns and the singers' gallery that runs along the upper edge of the room. The candelabra are hung with the coats of arms of the Russian governors.*

74-75 *In the west part of the Winter Palace, the Gold Drawing Room was designed by A. Bryullov after the 1837 fire. With the elaborately decorated ceiling, the gilded walls make this room extremely sumptuous. Today it contains a collection of applied Western art.*

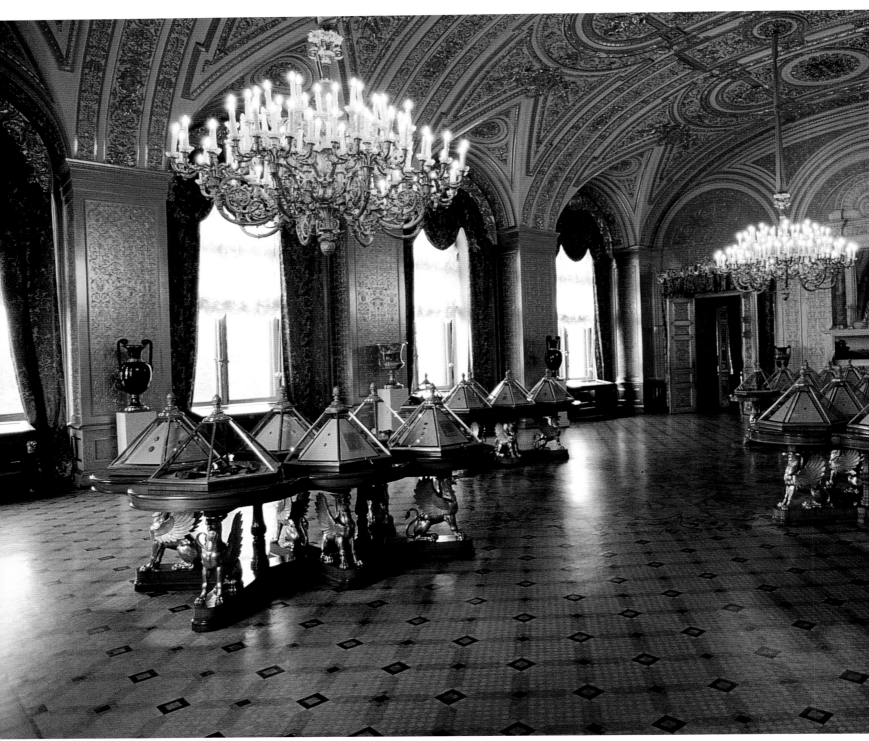

as in 1941 during the siege of Leningrad), and he had a New Hermitage built that was to be open to art lovers. The ten gigantic Atlantes made from grey granite that stand at the entrance to the new pavilion on Milionnaya Street were the work of Alexander Terebenev. On February 5, 1852, the first visitors entered the rooms designed by the great Neoclassical architect Leo von Klenze. Some rooms had been inspired by ancient Greek architecture. Others, like the three "Skylight" rooms, were illuminated from above to better display the paintings of the Italian and Spanish schools that hung on the red brick walls. Initially access to the gallery was closed at lunchtime so that Nicholas I could visit it, as he wished, each day. Furthermore, only men wearing uniform or tail-coats and women in court dress were allowed to enter but, at least, the museum had become a reality. Over the years that followed, all the sovereigns acquired new works in accordance with their personal taste, and masterpieces like the *Gonzaga Cameo*, *The Litta Madonna* by Leonardo da Vinci and the *Madonna Conestabile* by Raphaello were included. During the Soviet era, the fortunes of the Hermitage were often interwoven with the dramatic events taking place in the nation. Though the collections continued to be enlarged through the confiscation of private assets (e.g. the famous collection belonging to Prince Yusupov and those of the Muscovites Scukin and Morozov), numerous works ended up in the Pushkin Museum in Moscow

75 top left Only one work by Michelangelo Buonarroti is held in the Hermitage and is displayed in the center of this room. It is the Crouching Boy *that was carved for the Medici Chapels in Florence but then not included in the monument.*

75 top right The gallery owns a superb collection of fifteen sculptures by Antonio Canova (1757-1822) from different periods of his creative life. In the foreground there is the famous sculptural group Love and Psyche *from 1796.*

75 bottom The rooms of the Hermitage were decorated by outstanding masters with all the pomp due to an imperial palace but also provide a perfect setting for exceptional works of art. The photograph shows Threatening Love *by the French sculptor E.M. Falconet.*

and several masterpieces were sold abroad during the difficult 1920s and 30s. After climbing the Jordan Staircase, a visit to the Hermitage begins in the Small Throne Room (1833) designed by August Montferrand in honour of Peter I. The Military Gallery by Carlo Rossi was created in 1826 to celebrate the victory over Napoleon and to hang the three portraits of the allied rulers (Alexander I of Russia, Frederick William III of Prussia, and Franz I of Austria) and of the 332 generals who took part in the Patriotic War. The Heraldic Room (1839) covers more than 8600 square feet and houses a collection of European silver and an imperial carriage. The Throne Room, also known as St. George's Room, was designed by Quarenghi with white monolithic columns and linings made from Carrara marble. In 1906 it was the setting for the meeting of the first Duma (the Russian parliament).

The pavilion that looks onto the winter garden is truly enchanting. Its exquisite, sophisticated elegance in Eclectic style by Stakenschneider is mixed with elements from Moorish art, and the architecture of the Renaissance and antiquity. The small "fountains of tears" are inspired by those in

Bachcisarai Palace in the Crimea, the linings are in polychrome marble, the 28 chandeliers are all different in design, and the floor reproduces a mosaic from ancient Rome. The famous peacock clock made by the English master clockmaker James Coxe was a gift from Catherine II to her favorite, Prince Potemkin.

The spectacular Malachite Room was conceived by Alexander Bryullov in 1839 for Alexandra Feodorovna, the wife of Nicholas I, with columns and vases made from the green stone mined in the Urals, and with gilded doors and ceilings. During the attack on the Winter Palace on November 7, 1917, this was the room in which the guards brought an end to Kerensky's government.

The Council Staircase (crossed by members of the State Council on their way to sessions with the czar) leads down to the first floor where there are many magnificent creations by Russian stone-carvers. One is the malachite vase made in 1843 with the "Russian mosaic" technique, another is the famous work by Kolyvan which amazes with its formal beauty and perfection and its extraordinary dimensions (carved from a single block of jasper, it stands more than three feet high, its greatest diameter is more than eight feet, and it weighs 19 tons).

The six palaces of the Hermitage in fact only exhibit five percent of the museum's complete collections, which total almost three million items.

76 top Fruitstands, jugs, and condiment holders made from porcelain and precious metals are displayed in one of the rooms in the General Staff building that were part of the apartments used by Count Karl Nesselrode. The building was part of the expansion plans for the museum complex known as the "Great Hermitage."

76 bottom The Boudoir is located in the private apartments of the sovereigns in the west part of the Winter Palace. It was designed by A. Bryullov after 1837. The room's current appearance with red lining and a massive amount of gilt was originated in Stakenschneider's renovation and is typical of the eclecticism of the second half of the nineteenth century.

76-77 Nicholas II's study (his bust is in the foreground) and the Winter Palace library have managed to retain their original Gothic appearance designed by A. Krasovsky in 1894. The carved walnut ceiling, bookcases and furniture were produced by a famous furniture workshop in St. Petersburg.

77 top The Palladian style theater in the Hermitage was designed by G. Quarenghi, who was allowed a private box as a sign of gratitude from Empress Catherine. Members of the royal family often participated in performances and concerts were conducted by famous composers such as Paisiello and Cimarosa.

The prehistoric art section contains items discovered on the territory of the former Russian empire and magnificent jewellery produced by Scythian nomads (8th-3rd centuries BC), including a gold shield-plaque in the form of a deer, various animal-shaped brooches, and several gold objects found on Scythian territory but produced by Hellenic masters, for example, a splendidly decorated comb from the late fifth-early fourth century BC. In 1720, Peter the Great had already purchased the *Tauride Venus*, a sculpture from the second century BC that is one of the most important items in the Classical Art section. The museum also has an unrivaled collection of Attic vases decorated with red figures and magnificent cameos. The piece known as the *Gonzaga Cameo* (285-246 BC) is of inestimable value and was a gift to Alexander I from Josephine Beauharnais, Napoleon's first wife.

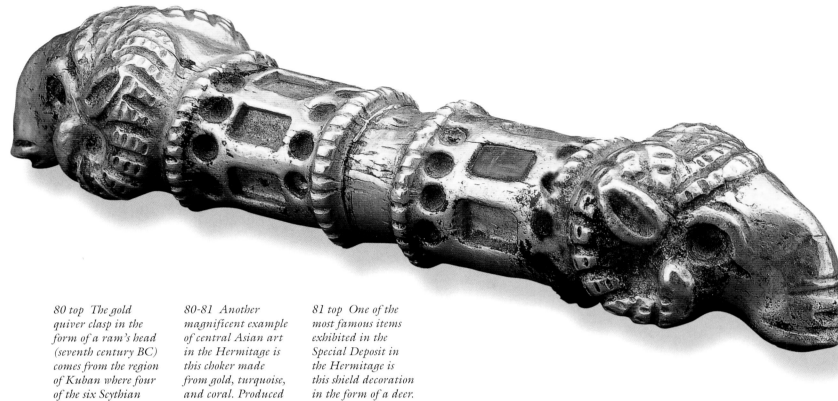

80 top The gold
quiver clasp in the
form of a ram's head
(seventh century BC)
comes from the region
of Kuban where four
of the six Scythian
tombs known today
were discovered in
1903.

80-81 Another
magnificent example
of central Asian art
in the Hermitage is
this choker made
from gold, turquoise,
and coral. Produced
in the fifth or fourth
century BC, it belongs
to the Siberian
collection of Peter I.

81 top One of the
most famous items
exhibited in the
Special Deposit in
the Hermitage is
this shield decoration
in the form of a deer.
It comes from Kuban
and dates from the
end of the seventh
century BC.

81 center and bottom
This gold vase was
produced by a Greek
craftsman in the
fourth century BC.
The main figure in the
decoration (center)
is a Scythian stringing
a bow. It probably
illustrates the myth
of the origin of this
people in which
someone injured his
mouth while preparing
his weapon, as the
scene seems to indicate.

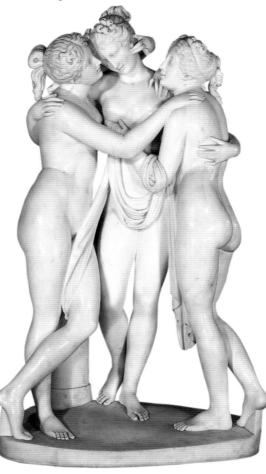

82 top left
Purchased in 1914,
the Madonna with
a Flower by
Leonardo da Vinci
(1452-1519) is one
of the most valuable
works of Italian art
in the museum. This
gentle and poetical
work was produced
in 1578 by the young
artist using the
new technique
of oil painting.

82 left bottom
The Lute player
(1595) is one of
Caravaggio's
greatest works and
the only one by
the painter in
the Hermitage.

82 right The Three
Graces by Antonio
Canova (1757-
1822) is one of the
fifteen masterpieces
by the Italian
Neoclassical sculptor
in the Hermitage.
This famous work
was produced
between 1812
and 1816.

83 The Litta
Madonna (1490)
once belonged to the
Italian dukes named
Litta and is one of
Leonardo da Vinci's
two works present in
the Hermitage. The
work is simple and
understated in its use
of color – with red,
blue, and black
predominating –
and transmits the
harmony and
interior beauty of
the two figures, the
Mother and Child.

However, although the Oriental and Russian art departments have works of great worth, it is the western art section that attracts the greatest number of visitors. It contains masterpieces like the *Judith* by Giorgione, *the Lute Player* by Caravaggio, *Amore and Psyche* and *The Three Graces* by Canova, the *Deposition* by Rubens (an artist represented by forty other works), the *Flora* and the *Return of the Prodigal Son* by Rembrandt, and *Portrait of a Woman* by Lucas Cranach the Elder. The European art section of the nineteenth and twentieth centuries holds a corpus of immense value with major artists such as Manet, Monet, Renoir, Degas, Van Gogh, Cézanne, Matisse, and Picasso all represented by some of their most famous works.

84 bottom The ten
works by Jean-Pierre
Renoir (1841-1919)
include the delicate
Portrait of the
Actress Jeanne
Samary (1878)
which came from the
Morozov collection in
Moscow. The artist is
unparalled in his
portrayals of women
and in the poetry of
feminine beauty.

84-85 Following
the nationalization
of the works of art
that belonged to the
rich after the
October
Revolution, the
collections of the
Hermitage were
enriched by many
nineteenth century
masterpieces such as
the Lily Bush by Van
Gogh (1889), one of
four of his works in
the Museum.

85 top
The Hermitage
owns one of the most
famous works by
Claude Monet
(1840-1926),
the master of
Impressionism.
It is the picture of
Jeanne-Marguerite
Lecandre in her
Garden.

85 bottom There are
many paintings from
the Tahitian period
of Paul Gauguin
(1848-1903).
One of the fifteen
in the Hermitage,
the Shepherdesses
of Tahiti is a rustic
scene set in the
innocent and
primitive paradise.

86 top left and 87 top The Hermitage possesses thirty paintings by Pablo Picasso. The Three Women *(86 left) and* Dance with Veils *(87 right)* represent his most famous phase – Cubism – in which the artist concentrated on deconstructing form.

86 top right The works by Picasso in the Hermitage came from the famous Muscovite collections of Scukin and Morozov. The works in the St. Petersburg museum's collection cover all the periods of the Spanish painter, including the blue period in which the Child with dog was painted.

86 bottom This is one of the many views of Mont Sainte-Victoire painted by Paul Cézanne (1839-1906). The work was part of the Morozov collection and is one of eleven works by the artist in the Hermitage.

86-87 A jubilation of joy and movement, the large canvas The Dance *by Henri Matisse (1869-1954)* was part of the collection that belonged to S. Scukin. Scukin was an enthusiastic admirer of the French painter and commissioned several works from him. Now it is one of the most famous works in the Hermitage Museum.

88 top left Nevsky Prospekt is the long street on which the most elegant residences were built in the first two centuries of St. Petersburg's history, and later, shops, banks, and hotels. This busy street is the best one on which to follow the development of St. Petersburg's architecture from the eighteenth century to the early years of the twentieth century.

88 top right Nevsky Prospekt runs into the Square of the Insurrection where it ended but it was later extended as far as Alexander Nevsky Abbey. The square is the location of one of the city's railway stations, Moscow, which was opened in 1851.

88-89 This stretch of Nevsky Prospekt leads towards the Admiralty whose tower can be seen in the distance. It does not have buildings of any particular artistic interest but there is an inscription on the building at no. 8 that dates from the days of the Nazi siege of Leningrad. It is a warning to pedestrians of the danger on that side of the street during bombardments of the city.

89 bottom The Literary Café at no. 18 on Nevsky Prospekt is one of the most typical of St. Petersburg meeting places. In this long-established café, it is possible to breathe some of the nineteenth century atmosphere of the Wolf and Béranger café visited by Pushkin and other literati.

LITERARY SCENES OF THE CENTER – FROM NEVSKY PROSPEKT TO NEVSKY ABBEY AND SMOLNY CONVENT

Already the most famous Russian writer of the nineteenth century, Nikolai Gogol, author of *Dead Souls*, stated in his short story *Nevsky Prospekt* that there was no more beautiful place in St. Petersburg than this crowded avenue, which, according to Thèophile Gautier, represented a sort of summary of the entire city. The three miles of the street, that stretch from the Admiralty to Moscow Station before curving gently towards Nevsky Abbey, are completely lined by marvelous buildings, palaces of the nobility and churches.

The history of Nevsky Prospekt began in 1710 when Peter founded the monastery dedicated to the Prince of Novgorod on the left bank of the Neva in the place it was thought the Swedish army had been defeated in 1240. The new road was cut through the forest by Swedish prisoners and paved with tree trunks, and in 1738 was given the name Nevsky after the abbey to which it led. Already the main city street at the time, the Prospekt was lined by buildings as far as the river Fontanka that marked the city limits. In 1800 the street's wooden paving was replaced with stones, and banks and hotels appeared beside the residences and shops. Starting from the Admiralty end, the most unusual palace from an architectural viewpoint is the former Wollenburg bank (no. 9) that was built in 1912 with a facade resembling a Venetian

palazzo. Opposite, at no. 8, on the wall of a building adorned with friezes and masks, there is a dramatic inscription that records the 900-day siege of Leningrad: "Citizens! In the event of artillery bombardment, this side of the street is particularly dangerous." Number 18 is known as the former Café Wolf and Bèranger, i.e. the "Café Chinois", in which the poet Alexander Pushkin made the appointment with his second Danzas, on February 8, 1837, that led to the fatal duel with Georges D'Anthès to defend the honor of Pushkin's beautiful wife, Natalia. Today it houses the Literary Café which evokes the atmosphere of the late nineteenth century with antique furniture, etchings, and live chamber music concerts.

90-91 Important
cultural events have
taken place in the
small perfect theatre in
the Rococo and richly
decorated Jusupov
Palace, for example,
musical performances
by Liszt and Chopin,
vocal performances by
the singers Viardot
and Saliapin, and
poetry reading by
Blok, Esenin and
Mayakovskyj.

91 top left
Alexander Pushkin's
study has remained
exactly as it was on
the day of his death,
with an ivory
papercutter, a bell,
and an inkpot on the
desk. A Turkish sabre
hangs on the wall
and the bookshelves
contain some of the
writer's library of
more than 4500
volumes.

91 top right
The courtyard of
the house-museum of
Alexander Pushkin,
with a statue of the
great poet in the
center, is one of the
literary shrines of
Russia. Recently
renovated, it was
here that he died on
January 29, 1837,
following a duel to
defend the honor of
his wife.

90 bottom The main
stairway of the
Yusupov Palace – one
of the most beautiful
of the palaces on the
Moyka – was rebuilt
during the second
half of the nineteenth
century by Ippolito
Monighetti who gave
it a lighthearted
decoration of stuccoes
in the French style of
the era of Louis XIV.

Pushkin's house, now a museum, is one of Russia's literary shrines. It is located at no. 12 on the Moyka embankment where it crosses Nevsky Prospekt. On this stretch of water, one of the most attractive in St. Petersburg, there stands the famous palace that belonged to the Princes Yusupov who came from an old and very rich family. The columned building was built in Classical style in the mid-eighteenth century according to a design by Vallin de La Mothe and rivaled the imperial residences in magnificence (it still houses a theatre). In December 1916, it was the scene of a tragic and unique event when the monk and mystic Grigori Rasputin was drawn into a trap by the owner of the palace, Felix Yusupov, and other nobles, where he was seized and assassinated. The rooms on the ground floor where the crime occurred exhibit lifelike wax figures and, exiting the courtyard, you would almost swear you were watching as the dying Rasputin dragged himself towards the frozen river to flee his assassins.

Returning to Nevsky Prospekt near no. 17, stands the Stroganov Palace, a masterpiece of Russian Baroque designed by Rastrelli and built between 1753 and 1760. On the main facade that faces onto the Moyka, four white Corinthian columns, the family coat of arms, and other decorative elements stand out against the dark green walls, which were originally painted bright orange.

Opposite the Stroganov palace stands the blue building of the former Dutch church that is the first of a series of places of worship of different faiths which, having been built in the capital of an Orthodox empire, demonstrate a remarkable religious tolerance for the period. A little further on, on the north side, there is the Lutheran church of the Apostles Peter and Paul, the Baroque Catholic church of St. Catherine (nos. 32-34) designed by Vallin de La Mothe, and the Armenian church designed by Yuri Felyten in 1780.

Further ahead on the other side of the road the Orthodox faith is represented in all its magnificence by the Neoclassical cathedral of the Virgin of Kazan, dedicated to the miraculous image of the Madonna. Paul I had wanted the cathedral to be a reproduction on a smaller scale of St. Peter's in Rome, with its superb colonnades.

However, the architect, Voronikhin, commissioned by Alexander I to design the building, produced an original work with a large dome the construction of which marked the first use of iron trusses. The cathedral, consecrated in 1811, looks onto Nevsky Prospekt over an impressive hemicycle bounded by 144 Corinthian columns. Low reliefs at the sides of the portico are sculpted with biblical motifs by Ivan Martos and Ivan Prokofiev while the niches contain bronze figures of Princes Alexander and Vladimir Nevsky, John the Baptist, and the apostle Andrew.

The cathedral's bronze doors are copies of the Doors of Paradise of the Baptistery in Florence. Two statues of war heroes from 1812 – Marshals Kutuzov and Barclay de Tolly – emphasize that the building is one of the most spiritually and politically significant places in Russia. In June 1813, Kutuzov was buried in this church where the flags of Napoleon's Grande Armèe and the keys of the forts conquered commemorate the Patriotic War. The interior of the cathedral, with 26 pink granite monolithic columns, is also adorned with a manycolored mosaic floor and frescoes painted by famous artists such as Vladimir Borovikovsky, Orest Kiprensky, and Karl Bryullov.

After the cathedral, Nevsky Prospekt crosses the Griboedov canal on which the Book House faces. This is a lovely modern building (1904) that used to belong to the American Singer sewing machine company before 1917.

From this point, there is a superb panorama of the canal which, until 1923, was called Ekaterinsky Canal (Catherine's Canal) and of the multicolor church of the Resurrection that closes the view. The church is similar in form to St. Basil's in Moscow but without that church's grace and lightness. It was built in pseudo-Russian style on the spot where Alexander II was assassinated on March 13, 1881. Construction of the highly ornate church took from 1887 to 1907 and the result, even if it is a little anachronistic in the context of the architecture of the city, is dramatic with its domes of changing colors, the *kokosnik* gables, the majolica tiles, and the more than 20 different semi-precious stones and marbles, including jasper, rodonite and porphyry used in decoration.

If you wish to stroll along the canal, past the magnificent suspension Bank bridge on which winged griffins hold up the cables, and past the Egyptian bridge adorned with bronze sphinxes, it is worth continuing as far as the Kryukov canal. This is one of the most magical points in St. Petersburg. It is dominated by the superb bell-tower of the Baroque church of St. Nicholas of Sailors, and is associated with the plot of one of Dostoyevsky's works, *White Nights*.

Moving away from this "literary" setting, you come to the city's temple of music, the green and white Marinsky Theater built in 1860 by Albert Kavos but then remodeled a few years later in Neo-Renaissance style. The outstanding auditorium is embellished by sumptuous sculptural decoration and a painted ceiling of slender, dancing muses. The superb curtain was decorated by Alexander Golovin in 1914, during the era of the great Russian ballet with dancers like Vaclav Nijinsky, Anna Pavlova and Tamara Karsavina, and the choreographer Michail Fokine, all of whom were part of the Marinsky company. Today the theatre has returned to international fame.

94 top The building that currently houses Marinsky Theater – the most famous in §the city – was built between 1859 and 1860 and dedicated to Alexander II's consort, Empress Maria.

94 center and bottom A performance of ballet is being given at the Marinsky. The Frenchman Marius Petipa, who arrived in Russia in 1847, brought international fame to its ballet corps.

94-95 The interior of Marinsky Theater shines resplendenty with the imperial box and Italian ceiling designed by Duzzi and painted by Fracioli. The huge chandelier is especially impressive. It was inspired by the crown of Monomaco and was the donation of a rich merchant.

96 top left
The Russian Museum holds many tours de force. The Last Day of Pompeii *by Karl Bryullov hangs on the right wall of this room. Bryullov was one of the most important Russian painters of the nineteenth century.*

96 top right The White Room is one of the most elegant in the Neoclassical Michailovsky Palace where the Russian Museum is housed.

96 bottom Built at the end of the nineteenth century, the Grand Hotel Europa is the most luxurious in St. Petersburg. It has recently been renovated to recreate the atmosphere of its original epoch.

Once back on Nevsky Prospekt, you come to the large yellow Grand Hotel Europa, built in 1873-1875, the most elegant hotel in the city. The entrance to the hotel is in the short Michailovskaya Street, at the end of which you will see the attractive facade of the Michailovsky Palace, (1819-1825) that used to belong to the younger brother of Alexander I, Grand Duke Michail Pavlovitch, and which is now home to the Russian Museum. To reach the building – one of the most successful examples of Carlo Rossi's Classicism – cross the Arts' Square in the center of which stands a monument to Pushkin by the sculptor Michail Anikusin, inaugurated in 1957. As the name suggests, the square, designed by Rossi in Neoclassical style, is effectively a hymn to the arts: opposite the museum stands the St. Petersburg Philharmonica, and on the west side there is the Mussorgsky Ballet and Opera House designed by Albert Kavos and built in the mid-nineteenth century. The Michailovsky Palace has a main body flanked by two wings that form a large courtyard closed by an elegant gateway. The *piano nobile* is decorated by a Corinthian portico with eight columns and by a pediment with low reliefs by Vasily Demut-Malinovsky and Nikolai Pimenov. Rossi also designed the interiors of the building, notable features being the double-ramp stairway and the White Room. The latter is a magnificent room that still has its original wood carvings, parquet floors, statues, and furniture intact. After the death of the Grand Duke, the efforts of his widow, Elena Pavlovna, turned the palace into a cultural and artistic center in which the famous pianist Arthur Rubinstein performed in the last century, but it was only in 1895 that Nicholas II bought it so he could use it to form

96-97 The statue of Alexander Pushkin stands in the foreground of the garden in front of the Corinthian portico of Michailovsky Palace. The statue by M. Anikusin was inaugurated in 1957.

97 top left The Russian Museum has a collection of 6000 icons, perhaps Russia's best-known form of art. The collection represents

all the iconographic schools of the country, in particular those of Novgorod, Moscow and the Stroganov school.

97 top right The Russian Museum was opened in 1898 by Nicola II and dedicated to Alexander III. It has over 380,000 works that describe the history of art in Russia from the tenth century to the present.

the museum dreamed of by his father, Alexander II, to house his large art collection. Opened in 1898, the Russian Museum was already too small to hold all of the collection so that Leonti Benois constructed a new wing for it from 1914 to 1919, which extended west as far as the Griboedov canal.

Today the Russian Museum spreads between buildings like the lovely Marble Palace, Stroganov Palace, and the Michailovsky Palace. It holds more than 350,000 examples of Russian art, one of the largest collections in the world. Icons are a particular feature

with masterpieces such as the *Apostle Paul* and the *Apostle Peter* by Andrei Rublev and Daniil Cerny from the early fifteenth century, *St. George and the dragon* by the Novgorod school from the second half of the fifteenth century, the *Odigitria Madonna* (c. 1500) by Dionisy, and the *Old Testament Trinity* by Simon Usakov (1671). Then come items of Russian art such as eighteenth century portraits and genre works on social and religious themes plus landscapes by the best known painters of that period, for example, Vasily Tropinin, Aleskei Vene-

98 The walk by Marc Chagall (1887-1995) is one of the painter's best works. He trained in St. Petersburg but then moved to Paris. The painting is in the dreamlike style that transfigures memory. It shows Chagall and his beloved wife Bella who fly in the sky over the houses and church of their hometown, Vitebsk.

cianov, Nikolai Ge, Ivan Aivazovsky, Vasily Polenov, Isak Levitan, and Karl Bryullov with the dramatic *Last Day of Pompeii* (1830-1833). A number of works by the best-known of the itinerant painters, Ilya Repin, represented by the famous *Boatmen on the Volga* (1870-1873), are held here. The collections that cover the late eighteenth and early nineteenth centuries are magnificent with avant-garde works by unsurpassed painters such as Malevitch, Filonov, Larionov, Goncarova, Kandinsky, and Chagall. Popular and decorative Russian art is also part of the collection, with lacquer boxes, wooden furniture, clothing, woven items, and clay toys. Finally, the right wing of the Michailovsky Palace houses the curious and interesting collections of the Ethnographic Museum dedicated to all the peoples that make up the mosaic of the former Soviet Union.

100 top The cheerful atmosphere of the large Art Nouveau style shop Gastronom Eliseev, dating from 1907, is evident in this photograph. Spiral columns, stained glass windows, sculptures, and large chandeliers give this temple of food and drink the appearance of the interior of a theater.

100 center The gable of Grands Magasins Gostiny Dvor bears the dates of its creation, 1761-1785. It was financed by the rich merchants of St. Petersburg. A single-story wooden shopping center of the same length used to exist on the same site in the early years of the city.

The building of the former Municipal Duma stands on Nevsky Prospekt opposite the Michailovsky Palace. It was designed by Quarenghi in 1784 and had a fire lookout tower added the following century in which an optical telegraph was installed to maintain contact between the Winter Palace and Czarskoye Selo, the czar's summer residence thirty kilometres from the capital.

The next block contains the majestic Neoclassical complex of the Gostiny Dvor with two-story arcades designed by Vallin de La Mothe (1761-1785). Intended to be a shopping area today is the largest commercial center in St. Petersburg. The south eastern facade of the building faces onto Sadovaya Street and the tree-lined Ostrovsky Square that is dominated by the statue of Catherine the Great (1873). Made from black granite, the figure of the czarina is shown in all her majesty with the most eminent individuals from her reign on the base. The square is dedicated to the playwright Alexander Ostrovsky. To the west it is bounded by the Saltykov-Schedrin Library by Carlo Rossi which contains twenty seven million books, manuscripts, and recordings. To the south stands the Alexander Theater, also by Rossi. Crowned by the two-wheeled chariot of Apollo, the elegant facade of the building faces Nevsky Prospekt, while the back of the theater forms the conclusion to St. Petersburg's most per-

fect street, named after its creator, the architect Carlo Rossi. The proportions of the street are perfect: it is 72 feet wide, and 720 feet long.

To the east of Ostrovsky Square there is the vast complex of Anichkov Palace, one of the first buildings to stand on Nevsky Prospekt. It belonged to Count Alexei Razumovsky, husband of empress Elizabeth. The building has undergone substantial alterations over the centuries but certain sections have been conserved as they were during the era of the czars.

On the other side of the street there is an Art Nouveau palace built in 1907 for the Eliseev brothers. It is the location of the food and wine shop of the same name, the most famous and elegant in the city. The palace contains the Theater of Satire in a mixture of commerce and art typical of this street.

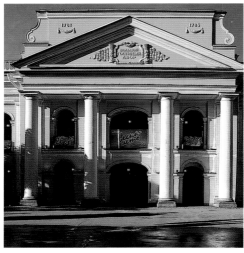

100 bottom Rossi Street bears the name of the great architect who designed all the surrounding district. This street has perfect proportions and is rightly considered the loveliest in St. Petersburg.

101 The architectural layout of Ostrovsky Square was also the work of Carlo Rossi, who designed the Neoclassical Alexander Theater between 1828 and 1832 with a roof crowned by Apollo's two-wheeled chariot. The monument (1873) dedicated to Catherine II can be seen in the foreground.

103 top left The four bronze sculptural groups that adorn the ends of Anichkov Bridge represent four phases in the taming of horses. In a city often subjected to disastrous flooding, these symbolize man's struggle with the elements and are a good interpretation of the spirit of St. Petersburg.

102 top Seremetev Palace was where the poet Anna Akhmatova lived from 1924 to 1952 and is now a museum dedicated to her. The palace was built around the mid-eighteenth century by Count Peter, son of one of Peter the Great's general, who called it the "House of Fountains." The architect who designed it was Savva Tchevakinsky, one of Rastrelli's pupils.

102 bottom A reminder of the city's marine vocation, this detail on the cast iron decoration of Anichkov Bridge shows the fantastic figures of two seahorses and, in the middle, Neptune's trident, one of the recurring symbols in the city.

102-103 Anichov Bridge over the river Fontanka along Nevsky Prospekt was built from stone between 1783 and 1785 to a standard model and rebuilt in 1841.

Anichkov Bridge carries Nevsky Prospekt across the river Fontanka and is unrivaled in its beauty. It was built by Peter I and was for half a century the official entrance to St. Petersburg. It was later to mark "the frontier" of the most elegant and aristocratic area in this lively street, the section that extended between the Admiralty and the Fontanka. Originally made from wood, in 1841 a wider version of the bridge was rebuilt in granite by Karl Schinkel. It was embellished by four bronze equestrian sculptures known as the *Horse tamers* by Petr Klodt. Following the Fontanka in the direction of the Neva, where the aristocracy's country houses used to stand in the first half of the eighteenth century, you will see the Baroque Seremetev Palace of 1712 at the end of a courtyard closed by an elegant gate. The building was a lively meeting place for artists (Franz Liszt was one of its frequenters) and is now the home of the Music Museum. Under the Soviets, it was the home of the poetess Anna Akhmatova, to whose memory and poetry the building is now indissolubly linked.

Further on, washed by the river Moyka, stands one of the city's most curious buildings, the red Michailovsky, or Engineers', Castle built in 1797-1801 by Vasily Bazhenov and Vincenzo Brenna. Paul I, the son of Catherine II, was both a lover of the Middle Ages and obsessed by the idea of a conspiracy so he had this building constructed for his own protection. It was defended by

moats, drawbridges (no longer in existence), thick walls, slit windows, secret passages, and maze-like corridors. Nonetheless, all these precautions were of no use because Paul I, was assassinated there on March 11, 1801. The name "Engineers' Castle" is derived from the institute that was based in it and whose most famous student was Fedor Dostoyevsky. The equestrian statue of Peter the Great by Rastrelli stands in the entrance to the castle.

In 1714, Peter had Domenico Trezzini build an imperial summer residence on the banks of the Fontanka. Conserved almost intact in its original Dutch style, the palace stands on the site of the Summer Garden, which the emperor requested be created in Italian style and surrounded by water. As a result, the complex lies among the Neva, the Moyka, the Fontanka and the poetic Swans' Canal. The Fontanka river was named after the fountain in the park which was fed with its waters before the destructive flood of 1777. During the summer, the garden, surrounded by a very elegant eighteenth century railing, is a refuge from the heat, with tall trees, flowerbeds, the Tea and Coffee Houses, and statues made from white marble.

103 top right *Another monument to Peter the Great, this time shown as a triumphant Roman emperor, stands opposite the nineteenth century Michailovsky Castle by Vasily Bazhenov and Vincenzo Brenna. Cast in 1747, the bronze equestrian statue by B.C. Rastrelli (the father of the famous architect) was only installed in this square many years later.*

104 top The sumptuous dark red Baroque facade of Beloselsky-Belosersky Palace is adorned with caryatids that support the columns they are set into. Designed in 1848 by A. Stakenschneider, the building was later lived in by Prince Sergei Alexandrovitch, the governor of Moscow who was assassinated during the 1905 revolution.

104-105 The large monastic complex named after Alexander Nevsky, which bears the distinguished title of lavra indicating an important orthodox monastery, dates from 1710. The red and white church of the Annunciation is the oldest in the complex (1717-1722) by Domenico Trezzini. It is a sort of Pantheon that contains the tombs of great individuals from the age of the Empire.

105 top left
The Nevsky Abbey enclosure wall was built in 1785 and gives the complex the appearance of a fort. Inside the wall there are seven churches and three graveyards.

105 top right
Michail Kozlovsky produced this statue of Alexander Suvarov in 1801. Suvarov was of one of Russia's greatest generals and marshals during the first Napoleonic War; here he is shown as Mars, the god of war. The shield with the Russian emblem protects the papal tiara and the crowns of the kings of Naples and Sardinia.

105 center
The eternal flame burns in the huge square northeast of St. Petersburg from which the main avenue in Piskarevskoye cemetery departs. This is where the victims of the German siege from 1941 to 1944 were buried in large common graves. The pavilions of the memorial built in 1960 contain a documentary exhibition dedicated to the terrible sacrifice of the city.

Next to the Summer Garden there is a large park called the Field of Mars. As the name suggests, it was intended to be used for military exercises and was so sandy it was known as "the Sahara of St. Petersburg." In 1801 the Field of Mars was the site of a monument to the Russian general, Suvarov, but this was later moved closer to the Neva. The site was then transformed into a garden before becoming a war memorial and cemetery with 184 graves of the dead from the February Revolution and a perpetual flame in a granite monument. The large yellow building with white colonnades to the west (1817-1822) was designed by Vasily Stasov for the guards of the Pavlovsky regiment. Retracing back to the Nevsky Prospekt, next to the Anichkov Bridge, stands the Beloselsky-Belozersky Palace designed by Stakenscheider in 1848. Its dark red facade with Baroque caryatids and columns is reflected in the waters of the river. The next stretch of the street, known as Old Nevsky, has no particular artistic interest with the exception of the abbey at the end in Alexander Nevsky Square. The large monastic complex is one of the four main Orthodox abbeys in Russia and the Ukraine. It is surrounded by a thick enclosure wall from 1785 and contains seven churches and three cemeteries. St. Lazarus' graveyard was founded by Peter the Great and contains the tombs of many famous architects that helped build the city – Starov,

Zacharov, Thomas de Thomon, Voronikhin, Quarenghi, Stasov, and Rossi – while Tichvin graveyard is where writers, painters and composers are buried, with the graves of Dostoyevsky and Tchaikovsky. Nikolsky cemetery is where the dead from World War II were buried.

The oldest building in the monastery is the red and white church of the Annunciation designed by Domenico Trezzini. It is a mausoleum of great figures of the Empire and the one that Catherine II chose as the last resting place of her husband Peter II.

The Neoclassical cathedral of the Trinity, (Ivan Starov, 1790) stands out from the other Baroque buildings for its twin towers, its portico with six Doric columns, and its pediment decorated with gilded reliefs. The highly elaborate interior includes a marble iconostasis with copies of works by Rubens, Van Dyck, Perugino and Reni, and the altarpiece is by Anton Raphael Mengs. The superb silver reliquary that holds the remains of Alexander Nevsky once stood in the cathedral but is now in the Hermitage.

The other famous monastic complex in St. Petersburg is the Smolny. Commissioned from Rastrelli by Elizabeth I, who wished to retire to a convent during the last years of her life, construction of the complex began on the large bend of the Neva in 1748. However, Catherine II was not a great lover of Baroque architecture and dismissed the Italian from the job but, in 1835, the cathedral was completed by Stasov in accordance with the original plans and today remains a masterpiece. The ornamental exuberance of the Baroque seen in this white and turquoise form integrates perfectly with the traditional gilded "onion-shaped" domes of Russian churches.

Not far from the monastery stands the severe, Neoclassical, and imposing Smolny Institute, designed by Quarenghi (1806-1808). It is not famous for having been the site of the Institute at which the daughters of the nobility were educated until August 1917, but for having become the seat of the Soviet deputies, workers, and soldiers of St. Petersburg in the same year. With Lenin at its head, the council remained in the palace until March 1918 when it was transferred to Moscow along with the capital of the USSR. Today the

106-107
The convent of the Resurrection, more commonly known as Smolny, has an almost fairytale beauty in its characteristic and harmonious colors of blue, white, and gold. The name Smolny comes from the deposits of tar (smola in Russian) that lie on the large bend of the Neva to the east of the city center where the complex was built for czarina Elizabeth.

Smolny is the site of the City Council. The name Smolny was derived from the works that produced the tar (*smola* in Russian) used to caulk the ships around the area from the times of Peter the Great.

Yet another elegant aristocratic residence in the area, one of the first Russian constructions in Classical style, and modeled on the Pantheon in Rome, it was involved in the revolutionary events. The Tauride Palace is adorned with a Doric gable topped by a green dome. Catherine had it built by Starov (1783-1789) for Prince Potemkin, the hero of a victorious military campaign against the Ottomans in the Crimea ("Tauride" is the Greek name for the Crimea). Following a series of changing fortunes, at the time of the February revolution the building was used by the Soviets and committee of the Duma to organize the Provisional government. Built as an imperial city, St. Petersburg became instead the cradle of the revolution. Now, at the start of the new millennium, it is once more discovering its former magnificence but in a new dimension, modern but not forgetful of its complex, contradictory, and sometimes dramatic history and its unique architectural heritage.

107 top Tauride Palace was a present from Empress Catherine II to Prince Potemkin who, in 1783, won back the Crimea from the Turks. The building is among the greatest triumphs of Ivan Starov, one of the heads of the Russian Neoclassical school. The main portico of the facade is embellished with simple white Doric columns that met the anti-Baroque tastes of the czarina perfectly.

107 bottom Smolny Institute – to the south of Smolny Convent – was built by Giacomo Quarenghi and housed the college that educated the daughters of the aristocracy until 1917. The main entrance has a large, eight-column portico crowned by a broad gable. In 1917 it became the offices of the leadership of the October Revolution and today is the seat of the Municipality.

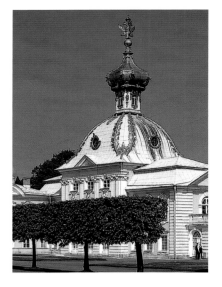

PETERHOF:
THE GLORY AND TRIUMPH

108 top right The Baroque Pavilion of the Imperial Eagle in the Great Palace was designed by Rastrelli (1745) and takes its name from the gilded emblem of the Russian empire on the dome.

108 bottom left The most interesting fountain in the Upper Park is that of Neptune, which was purchased in 1799 in Nuremburg by Paul I before he became emperor. The figure of the god of the sea stands on a high pedestal, surrounded by Nymphs, seahorses, and their riders, and putti *on dolphins and sea dragons.*

O f the summer residences built around St. Petersburg by the Russian imperial family, Peterhof, the first, is the most appealing for its unusual position on the seaside and the manner in which it reflects the extraordinary personality of its constructor whose name it bears, Peter the Great. It was the "sailor" or "carpenter" czar (nicknamed after his personal interests) who chose the site and laid down the general lines of the project: the Upper Garden, Lower Park, the Great Palace, and the ingenious system of fountains and waterfalls that was facilitated by the lie of the land which sloped down towards the Gulf of Finland in terraces. After the foundation of the new capital, St. Petersburg, Peter I had conceived the notion of creating a collection of palaces, similar to those he had visited in France, around the new city. Peterhof was called the "Russian Versailles" but the seaside residence

has a very definite character and does not in fact have much in common with the French palace of the Sun King. In 1705, during construction of Kronstadt fort on the island of Kotlin in the Gulf of Finland, in order to reach the Peterhof building site more easily, Peter wanted a wooden house built on the seashore (this was later replaced by the Monplaisir pavilion, built in Peter's favorite Dutch style). The zone was rather wild and consequently in 1714 the ruler decided to make it more habitable by building a palace. It was officially opened in 1723 but Peter was never to live in it as he preferred the simpler pavilions in the park. One of these was called "Marly," like the one belonging to Louis XIV. At the time, European art was flourishing and to produce the ambitious project he had set down in innumerable sketches, he called the best foreign architects to St. Petersburg: the Frenchman Jean-Baptiste Leblond (a pupil of Andrè Le

108 bottom right Following the line of the Maritime Canal from the terrace of the Grand Cascade, the view stretches as far as the Gulf of Finland.

109 The long body of the Great Palace of Peterhof separates the Upper Garden (in French style with fountains, statues, and symmetrical flowerbeds) from the wooded Lower Garden crossed by the Maritime Canal.

110 and 110-111 With gold reflections, the Grand Cascade is fed by 64 fountains and adorned with 225 gilded bronze sculptures that represent sea gods, Russian rivers, and the empire's marine commitment.

Notre, who designed the grounds of Versailles), the German Johann Friedrich Braunstein, and the Italian Nicolò Michetti. The latter two designed the Great Palace in Baroque style that stands on a natural terrace 53 feet high and separates the Upper Garden from the Lower Park. The building overlooks the Grand Cascade, the fantastic masterpiece of this complex which endows Peterhof with a unique and unmistakable character. The current appearance of the Palace is the work of Bartolomeo Rastrelli

who raised the central section of the building by one floor and built two low wings at the sides, each terminating in a pavilion, during the reign of Peter's daughter, the empress Elizabeth I. The pavilion to the east is the Chapel with five, "onion-shaped," gold domes. To the west is the pavilion "below the coat of arms," so-called because a two-headed eagle crowns the dome. The 886 feet of its refined and elegant front facade faces the sea with white pillars, plinths, and window frames that stand out against its yellow body. The tranquil horizontality of the wings connects the main section, topped with a mansard roof, to the vertical lines of the two pavilions. The other side of the buildings has the same elegance and embraces the Upper Garden – in French style – in the center of which stands the spectacular Neptune Fountain, surrounded by horses, sea-horses, and dolphins. At

112 top left
The white walls of the Audience Room were designed by Rastrelli in Baroque style and were decorated with an abundance of gilded stuccoes. The large mirrors opposite one another create the optical effect of amplifying the magnificent interior.

112 top right Among the objects belonging to Peter the Great in his oak study were an inkpot, a travel pen, and an English globe. The furniture includes two elegant cabinets that hold small safes and look like miniature palaces. The study was designed by Leblond with carved wood paneling designed by Nicolas Pineau between 1718 and 1720.

112-113 The large Throne Room (roughly 3550 square feet) in Neoclassical style is decorated with portraits of the royal family. The throne of Nicholas I stands in the background. The delicate amethyst color of the crystal chandeliers (made in the factory of Prince Potemkin near St. Petersburg) was created by adding gold and other metals during melting.

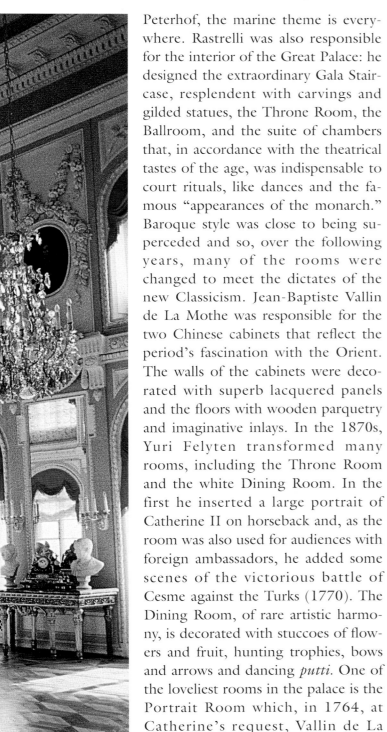

Peterhof, the marine theme is everywhere. Rastrelli was also responsible for the interior of the Great Palace: he designed the extraordinary Gala Staircase, resplendent with carvings and gilded statues, the Throne Room, the Ballroom, and the suite of chambers that, in accordance with the theatrical tastes of the age, was indispensable to court rituals, like dances and the famous "appearances of the monarch." Baroque style was close to being superceded and so, over the following years, many of the rooms were changed to meet the dictates of the new Classicism. Jean-Baptiste Vallin de La Mothe was responsible for the two Chinese cabinets that reflect the period's fascination with the Orient. The walls of the cabinets were decorated with superb lacquered panels and the floors with wooden parquetry and imaginative inlays. In the 1870s, Yuri Felyten transformed many rooms, including the Throne Room and the white Dining Room. In the first he inserted a large portrait of Catherine II on horseback and, as the room was also used for audiences with foreign ambassadors, he added some scenes of the victorious battle of Cesme against the Turks (1770). The Dining Room, of rare artistic harmony, is decorated with stuccoes of flowers and fruit, hunting trophies, bows and arrows and dancing *putti*. One of the loveliest rooms in the palace is the Portrait Room which, in 1764, at Catherine's request, Vallin de La

Mothe turned into an unusual gallery, filling it with 368 paintings by Pietro Rotari of predominantly young women dressed in the traditional costumes of the fifty Russian territories. Study of the portraits, however, shows that the painter used only eight models. The suite of rooms used by the czarinas has splendid tapestries (almost all faithfully replicated during restoration of the site following the almost total destruction the palace suffered during World War II), like the one from Lyons in the Partridge Room. For artistic and historical reasons, the silk that lines the walls in the Crown Room is very important, showing all the details in scenes of the then highly secret process of producing porcelain. It is the fountains that play a fundamental role at Peterhof and give the complex its unique character. The symbol of a new sea power, they were

113 top The Portrait Room by Leblond and Rastrelli contains 368 paintings that Catherine II purchased from the widow of Pietro Rotari, Elizabeth I's court painter. The paintings extol the grace of Russian women but, as a reminder of the transience of beauty, the face of an old woman appears several times.

113 bottom When the court was at Peterhof, the royal insignia were kept in the Crown Room on the small table designed by Brenna. The walls of the alcove are lined with eighteenth century Chinese silk and there is a carved and gilded wooden bed in the room.

114 top These Sèvres porcelain vases (1807) are kept in the Cottage in Alexander's park. The vases were a present from Napoleon I to Alexander I.

114 bottom Two tables in the Monplaisir Palace are laid out with the purplish red porcelain dinner set with gilt rims made by Gurevsky. The decoration was inspired by the people and costumes of Russia.

119 The walls of the Gala Staircase are covered by very fine decorations with garlands of flowers, vases, mythological figures, and false niches. Two bays containing gilded wooden statues of Autumn and Winter face the slender figures of Summer and Spring.

115-118 The Great Palace was designed in Baroque style by Leblond and Braunstein and later enlarged by Rastrelli. It is the hub of the Peterhof complex. The building overlooks the Grand Cascade, the loveliest of a series of fountains and pools that make Peterhof – Peter the Great's favorite residence – the most extraordinary of the imperial palaces.

fed by a system designed by an engineer named Tuvolkov with the help of the czar. The water arrived from the Ropscin hills 14 miles to the south, crossing several natural and artificial basins and many canals and locks on their way. Celebration of the victory over Sweden at the battle of Poltava in 1709 is the theme of the Grand Cascade. This is the most beautiful and striking fountain at Peterhof and has become its symbol. Even its position in the center of the Lower Park is significant, dominated from above by the Great Palace and joined to the sea by a canal to symbolize continuity. Another of the 64 fountains on the site is the "Samson Rending the Lion's Jaws" fountain from which a jet 66 feet high spurts and which the czar often compared to the biblical hero who defeated a lion. In another interpretation, Samson represents Russia and the lion Sweden because Peter I had defeated his enemy at Poltava on St. Samson's day. The charm of Peterhof – this extraordinary, fountain-filled garden close to the sea – almost seems to portray in a different light the emperor who was famous for his anger and cruelty. Here it was said, as someone said, Peter "showed he was not alien to what can only be called poetry".

CZARSKOYE SELO: THE PALACE OF ALL THE RUSSIAS

The marvelous palace of Czarskoye Selo is the "czar's village," an architectural jewel set in a vast park. It is closely linked to Catherine II, who preferred it to all others and transformed it to her tastes, but it was Peter I who chose the place to the south of the city and gave it to his wife Catherine.

The first construction was fairly simple and passed to Peter and Catherine's daughter, Elizabeth I, who decided to make it her summer residence upon her succession to the throne in 1741. Consequently, she invited the best Russian architects to design it for her. Unsatisfied by all the proposals, the capricious empress turned to Bartolomeo Rastrelli in 1749 and the Italian genius created a palace that was considered at the time to be the most sumptuous in Europe.

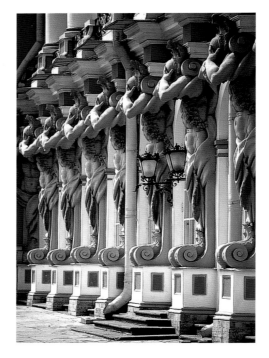

The Great Palace is a triumph of Russian Baroque architecture. It is a three story building with a 1066 foot long facade that ends in two pavilions: one contains the church with five golden domes, the other the main staircase.

Two wings spread from these elegant constructions that enclose a large courtyard closed by magnificent wrought iron gates. To avoid the monotony of such a large surface, Rastrelli enlivened the facade with protrusions and recesses and ornamented it abundantly with pillars and atlantes, columns, and statues, and alternating the light blue and turquoise colours with white and gold. The interior of the palace was especially lavish and, after World War II, was almost entirely renovated to its original splendor. It is

122 top In 1838, two sculptures of young boys by Pimenov and Loganovsky were placed in front of Alexander's Palace, a gift from Catherine II to her grandson and future czar, Alexander I.

122-123 Once called "The Morning Hall", the Grotto Pavilion by Rastrelli is a jewel of Baroque architecture. At the times of Catherine II it was used as a resting place during boat trips.

123 top left A detail of the gate in Catherine's Palace designed by Rastrelli shows the exquisite workmanship of the wrought iron, which has been transformed into golden lacework.

123 top right The building in the foreground, housed the former school at Czarskoye Selo, the most prestigious in all Russia, where Pushkin studied. Now the building is used as a museum.

123 bottom This romantic view of the grounds at Czarskoye Selo shows the blue and white bands of the well-proportioned Grotto Pavilion reflected in the tranquil waters of the Great Pond. In the distance and slightly higher, we see the Neoclassical Gallery designed by Charles Cameron with its semi-circular stairway and portico.

possible to follow the alterations made, mostly by Catherine the Great who, although a lover of Neoclassicism, ordered the Scot, Charles Cameron, to redesign the interiors in Baroque style. The Stairway from 1860, in which white is the predominant color, was the work of Ippolito Monighetti and leads to the reception rooms on the first floor. Of these, the Great Room is an example of the inimitable ostentation of the Russian court. The room covers 9257 square feet, is decorated in extravagant Baroque with mirrors, gilt, and on the ceiling, a painting of *The Triumph of Russia*.

The white and gold typical of Rastrelli triumph in the Knights' Room where the superb porcelain dinner services made for Catherine II by Gardner of Moscow are displayed. Two enormous majolica stoves – now only decorative – heated the room where the knights waited to be received by the sovereigns. The most mysterious and interesting story from the time of Peter I is linked to the celebrated Amber Cabinet. When in 1716 the czar visited Frederick William I of Prussia, he saw a room lined with panels made from fossilized resin and was so impressed that his host gave them to him. At first, the resin panels were used to ornament the Winter Palace in St. Petersburg and it was only in 1755 that they were taken to Czarskoye Selo. In 1942, German soldiers transferred the panels to Konigsberg, then, during their retreat, probably on to Germany where the valuable work of art disappeared. Even today, they remain the subject of an international mystery and fruitless search. The panels were made by Andreas Schluter in 1709 with thousands of pieces of amber and had rocaille

124 top left
The Salon is the
largest and most
luminous of the
Agate Rooms.
Colored marble
columns line the
walls and low reliefs
of mythological
subjects lie below
the arches. Two white
marble fireplaces are
adorned with low
reliefs: one is from
Italy and the other
is a copy of it made
in Russia.

124 top center The Agate Cabinet shines with the various bright and muted reds, whites, and greens of jasper. In the center of the room – divided into three sections by columns – there is a coffered ceiling. Porphyry vases stand on half-columns and the floor is made from palm, rosewood, and sandalwood to form an open umbrella.

124 top right The Cold Baths building on the first floor of the palace was designed by the Scot, Charles Cameron, between 1780 and 1787. It is known as the Agate Pavilion because of its beautiful lining in jasper mined in the Altai and Ural mountains. During the eighteenth century, jasper was known as "agate."

124-125 The Great Room or Ballroom is one of Rastrelli's masterpieces. At 9106 square feet, it is one of the largest rooms in the area of St. Petersburg designed by the master of Baroque. The room's volume is seemingly increased by the twelve enormous windows crowned by smaller ones.

style frames, also made from amber, that surrounded mirrors, medallions with the images of gods, and Florentine mosaics on the theme of the "Five senses of man." With the help of photographs, today this delicate work is being reproduced and has been partly completed.

In keeping with the decorative taste of the eighteenth century, Catherine's palace contained an art gallery so well-stocked that, hung beside one another, the works form a sort of "tapestry of paintings." They include pieces by Luca Giordano and Jean-Marc Nattier.

The green Dining Room marks the start of the apartment fitted out in the second half of the eighteenth century for Grand Duke Paul, the future emperor Paul I, Catherine's son. The decoration is rather unusual because only the walls are covered with low reliefs featuring white stucco figures

and tripods inspired by classical antiquity.

The Blue Room has original furniture designed by Cameron and is lined with a silk tapestry painted with floral motifs. In the Chinese salon, the silk linings have oriental motifs indicative of the eighteenth century interests of Europe and Russia in those exotic lands. The huge eighteenth century Chinese porcelain vases are also of great value.

The surprising bedchamber was used by both Paul's first and second wives and still preserves Cameron's original arrangement with the exception of a small renovation made by Vasily Stasov following a fire in 1820. With the exception of the grotesque sit-up baths, the dominating ornamental motif is a slender column of white porcelain around which gilded garlands are twisted. The plaster medallions with allegorical figures in

125 top The walls in the Picture Gallery are covered by a "tapestry" of 130 paintings by European artists purchased by Elizabeth I.

125 bottom The paintings in the Portrait Room include representations of nearly all the sovereigns in the Romanov dynasty linked to the history of Czarskoye Selo. The portrait of Catherine I, painted in 1725 by Adolisky, hangs on the left wall.

126 top left Large receptions were held in the Knights Dining Room, created by Rastrelli in 1750. The tables today are laid with the four dinner services of the Orders made in porcelain by the Gardner factory near Moscow in 1780. The gilded chairs were also designed by Rastrelli at the same time as the decorations.

126-127 The white Gala Staircase is highlighted with the gilt of the doors and the blues of the Chinese and Japanese vases. During World War II, the staircase was severely damaged but reconstruction began in the 1960s. Though elaborated by Monighetti, the stucco work was modelled on the original designs by Rastrelli.

127 top left Rastrelli's Amber Cabinet is lined with panels made from a mosaic of amber that are copies of the originals. They were a gift from Frederick William I of Prussia to Peter I but were stolen during the German siege of Leningrad and have never resurfaced.

126 bottom left Maria Feodorovna's bedchamber, designed by Cameron, is one of the most unusual rooms in the palace. He managed to combine intimacy with the luxury of the formal suites.

126 top center The two white marble putti on the landings of the main staircase symbolize two moments in the day: to the east the young boy wakes at dawn, to the west he sleeps at dusk.

126 top right This clock is one of the ornaments on the Gala Staircase in the center of the palace. Almost a century later, the staircase designed by Cameron was transformed into Rococo style.

relief are by the great Russian Classicist sculptor, Ivan Martos, and the combination of their light blue colour with the green of the walls provides a very refined chromatic harmony.

An elegant hallway was designed by Stasov with groups of Corinthian columns with gilded capitals and bases. It leads to Savva Tchevakinsky's Baroque Palace church from 1740 that features a six level iconostasis.

The marvels of Czarskoye Selo are also to be seen in the vast surrounding park which was one of the first English gardens in Russia. It includes pavilions, bridges and military memorials such as the Cesme column erected by Antonio Rinaldi in the middle of the lake. Designed by Rastrelli, the Baroque pavilion in the Hermitage – where Elizabeth loved to receive – had a dining room in which the table could be lowered and raised so that the food could be provided without the waiters disturbing the intimacy of the guests.

The manmade grotto with walls decorated with innumerable shells was first entrusted to Rastrelli but was later passed to Antonio Rinaldi by Catherine II, who kept her collection of objects made from semi-precious stones in a room there. An admirer of the Enlightenment and wishing to have a "Greco-Roman rhapsody in the garden at Czarskoye Selo," the empress invited Charles Cameron to Russia to build a covered gallery and Roman baths. Thus one of the most interesting complexes in the park,

built between 1783 and 1787, was conceived. The Cameron Gallery has a classical peristyle and Ionic columns, and the Frigidarium, used by Catherine for bathing and relaxation, is on the first floor of the Agate Pavilion, lined inside with jasper and malachite. Next to it lies the hanging garden.

One area of the park was set aside by Catherine for her favorite grandchild, the future Alexander I, where Alexander's Palace (Giacomo Quarenghi, 1792-1796) was built in classical style, with two rows of white Corinthian columns, and surrounded by buildings and bizarre Chinese bridges in line with the tastes of the period. This residence was especially loved by the last czars and, in 1905, Nicholas II and his wife Alexandra settled there permanently. It was from Alexander's Palace, where they were held under house arrest, that the whole imperial family was taken first to Siberia, then to Ekaterinburg where they met their tragic end.

The history of Czarskoye Selo is also closely associated with Russian literature because it was in the park and Catherine's palace that the famous school (now a museum) reserved for the children of the nobility was installed and where the great poet Alexander Pushkin studied. From 1937, the year that marked the centenary of his death, until a few years ago, the "czars' village" bore the name of Pushkin in honor of the great writer.

127 top right Music was played and friends entertained in the Gala Salon in the northern apartments of the building which belonged to Grand Duke Paul Petrovitch, the son of Catherine II, and his wife Maria Feodorovna. The profusion of mirrors, silk wall linings, lovely parquet floor, carvings, and gilded decorations designed by Cameron create an interior of captivating beauty.

128 top left The Rose
Pavilion takes its
name from the
rosebeds that
surrounded it. The
building is linked to
the memory of Maria
Feodorovna who liked
to entertain her
friends and guests
here. It was also the
setting for the joyous
but dignified meeting
on July 27, 1815
between Maria and
her son Alexander I
who had returned
from Paris after the
victory over Napoleon.

128 top right The
Temple of Friendship
was built between 1780
and 1782 for Paul, then
heir to the throne, in
honor of his mother
Catherine II and in
an attempt to improve
relations with her. This
was the first work by
Cameron at Pavlovsk
and the concept of
friendship is underlined
by the dedication at the
entrance and the
symbolism of the
decorative elements:
dolphins, crowns vines,
and leaves.

PAVLOVSK: BETWEEN NATURE AND REASON

128-129 Designed
by Cameron and
Brenna, the
Neoclassical palace
of Pavlovsk stands on
the banks of the river
Slavianka. With its
noble and stately
proportions, the
decoration of the
building is limited
to a severe and linear
portico and a few
reliefs. The central
body of the building
is crowned by a drum
surrounded by
columns and a low
dome. On either side,
semi-circular wings
extend to form a vast
court, in the center of
which (to the right in
the picture) stands
the statue of Paul I
by Ivan Vitali from
1851.

129 bottom
The Aviary designed
by Cameron in 1782
stands in the
southern part of
the grounds. The
colonnade covered by
nets contains many
species of birds.
A collection of
ancient objects,
bronze statuettes,
and ceramic vases
can be seen in an
adjacent area where
engraved marble
stones were later
added.

During the age of empress Elizabeth I, the vast, dense forest that almost touched Czarskoye Selo and that is traversed by the winding Slavianka river was one of the court's favorite hunting grounds. Here there were two wooden buildings, jokingly referred to as "creak" and "crack." Today, Pavlovsk, with its 1483 acres of land, is one of the largest parks in Europe, at the center of which stands a residence that belonged to and was named after Paul I. As a celebration of the birth of Paul's eldest child, Alexander, Catherine the Great gave this land to her son and his wife, Princess Maria von Wurtemberg (Maria Feodorovna in the Russian manner) where Charles Cameron was commissioned to build a palace. The Scot succeeded in harmonizing the Russian landscape with Classical architecture in his arrangement of the central section of the grounds, the Great Palace, and the first pavilions, including the famous Apollo's Colonnade dedicated to the Greek protector of the arts. When Paul I followed his mother to the throne, Pavlovsk became the official summer residence. The Italian architect Vincenzo Brenna built the Pil Tower on the bank of the Slavianka with a circular plan and conical roof. Outwardly, it appeared to be modest building but inside it was richly furnished and there was a miniature fort that held a small garrison and real cannons. At Maria Feodorovna's request, Brenna also made alterations to the palace. This was a pale yellow Palladian design with a dome supported by 64 white columns from which two galleries extended in a hemicycle. Brenna added a floor to the south gallery and two pavilions that he con-

130 The well-proportioned and elegant Italian Room is colored by the violet of the artificial marble, the gold of the bronze appliqués, and the pink of the rosewood doors. It occupies a central position in the palace. The austere symmetry is given a little relief by the alternation of vaulted and square niches topped by the elegant and slight balustrade of the singer's gallery.

131 top left The Lower Vestibule, designed by Cameron, is also known as the "Egyptian" Vestibule because of the style of the imposing allegorical statues that represent the months of the year. The sculptures are matched by the medallions of the signs of the zodiac on the walls.

131 top right Maria Feodorovna's bedchamber, designed by Vincenzo Brenna, can be described as "sumptuous." The large canopy bed decorated with allegorical sculptures of happiness and prosperity stands close to the silk lined walls painted with pastoral motifs. Other items of furniture, like the chairs, were the work of the famous French cabinet-maker Henri Jacob.

nected with curved wings to create a closed courtyard in the center of which stood a statue of Paul I. The best artists and architects of the era worked on the interior of the residence – including Giacomo Quarenghi, Carlo Rossi (who began his extraordinary career here), and Andrei Voronikhin (who rebuilt the palace after the fire of 1803).

Before Paul became emperor, he had traveled in Europe with his wife under the identities of "Dukes of the North," acquiring valuable works of art which, with presents from various rulers, were sent to furnish the palace being constructed.

It was an era in which the first excavation projects contributed to a great revival in the passion for antiquity. This is mirrored in the twelve large sculptures by Voronikhin in Egyptian style that symbolize the months and adorn the hall of Pavlovsk palace. There was also a Greek Room, a Neoclassical master-

piece by Cameron, and an Italian Room located below the central dome entirely painted to imitate marble. A tribute to the emperor's taste – he was fascinated by military art – were the two salons dedicated to War and Peace. Both are octagonal and lie respectively at the end of the suites of rooms belonging to Paul and Maria. They are decorated with low reliefs and gilding but in the Peace Salon, in place of weapons, there are cornucopias, garlands of flowers, musical instruments, and farm tools. The czar also named one room after the Knights who hid in Russia following Napoleon's siege of Malta, the Order of which the czar was made Grand Master. The architecture in the Knights of Malta Room is simple with pale green walls ornamented with white stuccoes and many sculptures, many of which were Roman.

Compared to other imperial residences, at Pavlovks there is a more "modest" atmosphere, as if it were

131 bottom left The Painting Gallery was designed by Brenna as a large semi-circular room in which the pictures were lit by large windows.

131 bottom right The Knights' Room was created by Brenna between 1797 and 1799. It was conceived as a gallery of ancient sculpture as well as a formal reception room. At the time it was built, Catherine II bought eight marble statues of the same size from the collection of an Englishman named Brown. The walls are entirely decorated by low reliefs.

132 top Pavlovsk palace suffered serious damage during World War II losing almost all its decorations. Only the original furniture and works of art were saved because they were removed in time. They were hidden in a remote area of the Urals during the war.

132-133
The original decoration of the Greek Room by Vincenzo Brenna was lost in the fire of 1803 but was later rebuilt by Voronikhin. The skillful use of plaster and sculptures, that reproduced the loveliest ancient works, combined with the elegance of the sixteen Corinthian columns in blue stucco form a tribute to the beauty of Greek art.

133 top The Throne Room is 4300 square feet in area and was initially planned to be a formal dining room. This function was celebrated in the low reliefs of fruit, flowers and musical instruments that decorate it. Today, the room's original purpose is emphasized by the famous dinner service expressly made by Guriev for the palace.

133 bottom left Reconstructed as it was at the start of the nineteenth century, the Common Studio was frequented by all of Paul I's family. The pictures on the walls include portraits of Maria Feodorovna and her nine children. Even the medallion in the center of the fireplace screen frames a drawing of the czar's wife.

133 bottom right The Upper Vestibule that leads to the Gala Staircase is the work of Brenna and the decoration, based on large stuccoes, is typical of his style. The theme is war and its symbolizm in various periods of history. Another unusual element are the plaster atlantes. The statue of Hercules on horseback originally stood near the Rose Pavilion.

simply a lovely house built for a numerous family (Maria Feodorovna had ten children) in which there was no lack of reception rooms. The largest of all, the Throne Room, designed by Brenna in 1797, was equipped for receptions and today it contains a gilded porcelain dinner set of over six hundred pieces. Particularly valuable are the blue Sèvres vases purchased in France by the czar. A magnificent toilette service also by Sèvres (a gift from Marie Antoinette) can be seen in Maria Feodorovna's *boudoir* which is decorated similarly to the Vatican loggias painted by Raphaello.

A sumptuous four poster bed stands in the empress's bedroom. The private apartments of the royal family on the ground floor offer a view of the simple daily life led by members of the family. They contain souvenirs, portraits, and sketches by Maria Feodorovna (who was artisti-

cally talented) while, in Paul's private study, there are many views of Gatchina Palace, his other residence.

Pavlovsk Park was chosen by Fedor Dostoyevsky as the setting for the most important scenes in his novel *The Idiot*, and here, the famous Italian painter Pietro Gonzaga worked to create "musical" harmony through the skillful arrangement of groups of trees, bushes, ponds, and meadows. Of the many pavilions, the Rose Pavilion is particularly associated with Maria Feodorovna, and her favorite flower, the rose, forms its dominating decorative motif. The Ballroom, designed by Gonzaga, was a later addition to the Rose Pavilion and was dedicated to Paul and Maria's son, Alexander, the "liberator of Europe." It was in this floral pavilion, where she loved to relax alone, that the empress welcomed her son on his return from the campaign against Napoleon.

INDEX

Please note:
c = caption
bold = dedicated chapter

A
Academy of Fine Arts, 57c, 59c
Academy of Sciences, 30, 56, 56c
Achilles, 60
Admiralty, **60-67**, 69, 89, 89c, 102
Adolisky, 125c
Aivazovsky, Ivan, 99
Ajax, 60
Akhmatova, Anna, 12, 102, 102c
Alexander I, 8c, 32c, 33, 33c, 35, 36, 60, 61, 62, 73, 75, 78, 93, 96, 114c, 122c, 126, 129, 129c, 133
Alexander the Great, 60
Alexander II, 38, 52c, 93, 93c, 94c, 96
Alexander Theater (or Alexandrinsky), 35, 100c
Alexander III, 38, 38c, 41c, 52, 96c
Alexander's Column, 8c, 35, 67, 67c
Alexandra, 126
Alexandra of Hesse, 41c
Alexandrovitch Vladimir, Palace of, 55
Alexandrovitch, Sergei, 104c
Alexandrovitch, Vladimir, 38
Alexandrovna, Maria, 52, 52c
Alexis, 42c, 50
Altman, Nathan, 99c
Amenhotep III, 59
Amiconi, J., 73c
Amsterdam, 22
Anastasia, Grand Duchess, 42c
Anhalt-Zerbst, Sophie von, 29, 29c
Anichkov Bridge, 10c, 22c, 49c, 102, 102c, 105
Anichkov Palace, 100
Anikusin, Michail, 96, 96c
Anisimov, 61c
Annunciation, Church of the, 104c, 105
Apollo, 100c
Apollo's Colonnade, 129
Arsenal, 50c
Artillery Museum, 50c
Arts' Square, 96
Ascension Prospekt, 25
Astoria-Angleterre, Hotel, 12c, 65
Aurora, cruiser, 8c, 44c, 45
Austerlitz, battle of, 32c
Austria, 20

B
Bachcisarai Palace, 70c, 76
Balaclava, battle of, 36c
Baltic Sea, 8, 20, 22, 44, 50
Basil Island (Vasilevsky Island), 22, **50-59**
Bazhenov, Vasily, 33, 102, 103c
Beauharnais, Josephine, 78
Beloselsky-Belozersky, Palace, 10, 10c, 104c, 105
Benois, Leonty, 98
Black Sea, 43c
Blok, Alexander, 10, 90c
Blue Bridge, 65, 65c
Bolsaya Morskaya Street, 65, 67c
Bonaparte, Napoleon I, 33, 35, 36, 61, 67, 73, 75, 78, 105c, 114c, 129c, 131, 133
Borovikovsky, Vladimir, 93

amstein, Johann Friedrich, 110, 4c
Brenna, Vincenzo, 33, 102, 103c, 113c, 129, 129c, 131c, 132c, 133, 133c
Bryullov, Alexander, 76, 76c
Bryullov, Karl, 62, 62c, 71c, 74c, 93, 99
Brodsky, Isaak, 44c
Brodsky, Josef, 8, 10, 12
Bruni, Fedor, 62, 62c
Brunnow, Count, 36c
Brutus, 29c
Buonarroti, Michelangelo, 75c
Byzantium, 120c

C
Cameron, Charles, 3c, 30, 30c, 122c, 123, 125, 125c, 126, 126c, 126c, 127c, 129, 129c, 131, 131c
Canova, Antonio, 75c, 82, 82c
Caravaggio, 82, 82c
Carrara, 52, 52c, 76, 102
Castor, 61
Catherine I, 24, 25c, 120c, 125c
Catherine II (the Great), 3c, 8, 27, 27c, 29, 29c, 30, 33, 33c, 35, 35c, 55, 56, 59, 60, 60c, 69c, 70, 73, 73c, 76, 77c, 100, 100c, 102, 105, 106, 107, 107c, 113, 113c, 120, 120c, 122c, 123, 125, 126, 127c, 129, 129c, 131c
Caucasus, 38
Cemesov, E., 27c
Central Asia, 38
Cerny, Daniil, 98
Cesme Church, 10
Cesme, battle of, 110
Cézanne, Paul, 82, 87c, 99c
Chagall, Marc, 98c, 99,
Chertomlyk, 79c
Chevakinsky, K. I., 136c
Chevakinsky, Savva, 56c, 102c, 120c, 126
Chopin, Frederick, 90c
Cimarosa, 73, 77c
Clinton, Bill, 48c
Collot, Marie-Anne, 60
Copenaghen, 38c
Count, Peter, 102c
Courland, 24
Coxe, James, 76
Cranach the Elder, Lucas, 82
Crimea, 38c, 70c, 76, 107, 107c
Crimean War, 36, 36c
Czarskoye Selo, Palace of, 3c, 12c, 27, 27c, 30, 30c, 36, 100, **120-127**, 129, 134c

D
D'Anthès, Georges, 89
D'Anthès, Natalya, 89
Danzas, 89
De Lemercier, 29c
de Thomon, Jean-François Thomas, 10c, 35, 56, 59c, 105
de Tolly, Barclay, 93
Decembrists' Square, 12, 60, 62
Degas, Edgar, 82
Delft, 59
Demut-Malinovsky, Vasily, 61c, 67, 96
Denmark, 21
Diderot, Denis, 29, 29c, 60
Dionisy, 98

Dnieper, 56
Dobrinsky, Count, 43c
Dostoyevsky, Fedor, 10c, 12, 50, 93, 102, 105, 133
Dunker, 120c
Duzzi, 94c

E
Eisenstein, Sergei, 43c
Ekaterinburg, 52, 126
Ekaterinsky Canal, 38c, 93
Eliseev, 100
Elizabeth I, 8, 25, 27, 27c, 29, 29c, 69, 69c, 70, 100, 106, 106c, 110, 113c, 120, 120c, 125c, 126, 129
England, 20, 36, 36c
Esenin, Sergei, 65, 90c
Ethnographic Museum, 99

F
Falconet, Etienne, 60, 75c
Feodorovitch, Michail, 38c
Feodorovna, Alexandra, 42, 42c, 76
Feodorovna, Maria, 126c, 127c, 129, 129c, 131, 133, 133c
Felyten, Yuri, 70, 90
Field of Mars, 10c, 105
Filonov, Pavel, 99
Finland, 44
Finland, Gulf of, 20, 22c, 30c, 48, 108, 108c
Fokine, Michail, 94
Fontana, Mario, 59
Fontanka River and Canal, 10c, 22c, 89, 102, 102c
Fracioli, 94c
France, 20, 32c, 35, 36, 36c, 133
Francis I of Austria, 76
Frederick William I of Prussia, 123, 126c
Frederick William III of Prussia, 75

G
Gapon, pope 40
Gardner, porcelain manufacturer, 123, 126c
Gatchina, Palace of, 133
Gauguin, Paul, 85c, 99c
Gautier, Théophile, 89
General Staff Building, 8c
Giordano, Luca, 125
Giorgione, 70, 82
Gogol, Nikolai, 10, 12, 89
Golovin, Alexander, 94
Goncarova, Natalya, 99
Gonzaga, Pietro, 133
Gorky, Maxim, 50
Gostiny Dvor, Grands Magasins, 100, 100c
Gotzkowski, 70
Grand Duke Michail, Palace of, 55
Grand Hotel Europa, 96, 96c
Great Hermitage, 55, 69c
Great Neva, 8c, 56
Griboedov Canal, 93, 93c, 98
Grimm, D., 52c
Gumilev, Nikolai, 12

H
Hare Island (Zayachy Island), 50
Hermitage Museum, 9c, 10, 13c, 50, 59, 67, **69-87**, 105, 126
Hermitage Theater, 27c, 30, 55, 73
Hitler, Adolf, 46, 47

Holstein-Gottorp, 29

I
Insurrection Square, 89c
Ivan V, 24c, 25
Ivanovna, Anna, 24, 24c, 27, 69

J
Jacob, Henri, 131c
John's Bridge, 50c

K
Kandinsky, Vasily, 99, 99c
Karelian Isthmus, 46, 61
Karsavina, Tamara, 94
Kavos, Albert, 94, 96
Kemiakin, Michail, 50, 51c
Kerensky, Alexander Feodorovitch, 45, 45c, 76
Kiprensky, Orest, 93
Kirov, Sergei, 45
Klenze, Leo von, 73c, 75
Klodt, Petr K., 10c, 65, 65c, 102
Kokorinov, Alexander, 59
Kolyvan, 76
Konigsberg, 123
Kotlin Island, 108
Kozlovsky, Michail, 105c
Krasovsky, A., 76c
Kronstadt, 46, 108
Kryukov Canal, 93
Kuban, 80c
Kunstkamera, 56, 56c
Kutuzov, 93
Kvasov, 120c

L
Ladoga, Lake, 10c, 22c, 46, 46c, 47, 69
Larionov, Michail, 99
Latvia, 24
Lazarus Cemetery, 10c
Leblond, Jean-Baptiste, 22, 56, 56c, 108, 113c, 114c
Le Notre, André, 22, 108
Lenin, Vladimir, 44, 44c, 45, 50, 67, 106
Leningrad, 45, 45c, 46, 46c, 47, 48, 73
Leonardo da Vinci, 75, 82c
Leopoldovna, Anna, 25
Levitan, Isak, 99
Lidval, Fedor, 12c, 65
Liszt, Franz, 90c, 102
Litta Dukes, 82c
Little Hermitage, 55, 67c
Little Holland, 65
Little Neva, 56
Livadia Palace, 38c
Livonia, 25c
Loganovsky, 122c
London, 22, 62c
Louis XIV, 90c, 108

M
Majakovsky, Vladimir, 90c
Malevitch, Kasimir, 99, 99c
Manet, Edouard, 82
Marble Palace, 55, 98
Maria of Wurttemberg, see Feodorovna, Maria
Maria, Empress, 94c
Maria, Grand Duchess, 42c
Marie Antoinette, 133

Marinsky Palace, 36, 65, 65c
Marinsky Theater, 35c, 94, 94c
Maritime Canal, 108
Martos, Ivan, 93, 126
Matisse, Henri, 82, 87c, 99c
Mendeleev, Dimitry, 59
Mengs, Raphael, 105
Menshikov Alexander, 25c, 59, 59c
Michael, Grand Duke, 37c
Michailovskaya, Street, 96
Michailovsky Palace, 33, 33c, 96, 96c, 98, 102, 103c
Michetti, Nicolò, 110
Middle Prospekt (Nevsky), 25
Milionnaya Street, 67c, 73
Military Gallery, 75
Mint, 55, 55c
Monet, Claude, 82, 84c
Monighetti, Ippolito, 90c, 123, 126c
Montferrand, Auguste de, 35, 62, 62c, 65, 65c, 67, 73c, 75
Morozov, 75, 84c, 87c
Moscow Station, 89
Moscow, 8, 20, 20c, 22, 24, 25c, 38, 45, 69, 89c, 93, 106, 123, 126c
Moscow, Pushkin Museum of, 75
Moyka River, 10c, 65, 65c, 90, 90c, 102
Mussorgsky Theatre, 96

N
Nachimov Naval Academy, 8c
Naples, King of, 105c
Nattier, Jean-Marc, 20c, 25c, 125
Naval Museum, 59c
Navy War Museum, 55, 56
Neptune Fountain 108c, 110
Nesselrode, Karl, 76c
Neva Gate, 52c, 55, 55c
Neva River, 8c, 10c, 12, 13, 20, 22, 24c, 25, 33c, 41c, 48, 50, 50c, 51c, 55, 56, 56c, 57c, 59, 59c, 60, 60c, 62, 65c, 67, 69, 69c, 70, 89, 102, 105, 106, 106c
Nevsky Abbey, 10c, 22, 23c, **89-107**, 93, 104-105c, 105
Nevsky Prospekt, 12, 22, 22c, 25, 46c, 88c, **89-107**
Nevsky Prospekt, 25
Nevsky, Alexander, 93, 104c, 105
Nevsky, Vladimir, 93
New Hermitage, 67c
Nicholas I, 12c, 36, 36c, 61, 62, 65, 65c, 69c, 71c, 73, 73c, 75, 76, 113c
Nicholas II, 38c, 40, 41, 41c, 42, 42c, 43c, 45c, 52, 76c, 96, 126
Nikolaevsky Palace, 36
Nikolsky Cemetery, 105
Novelli, P.A., 20c
Novgorod, Duke of (A. Nevsky), 89
Nijinsky, Vaclav, 94
Nystad, Peace of, 20

O
Odessa, 41, 43c
Olga, Grand Duchess, 42c
Orlov, Alexei, 24, 29, 36c
Orlov, Grigory, 55
Ostrovsky Square, 100
Ostrovsky, Alexander, 100

P
Paisiello, 73, 77c
Palace Square, 8c, 9c, 29c, 35, 67c
Paris, 8, 98c, 129c
Paul I, 29, 33, 33c, 60, 73, 93, 102,

108c, 125, 127c, 129, 129c, 131, 133, 133c
Pavlovitch, Costantino, 33c
Pavlovitch, Michail, 96
Pavlova, Anna, 94
Pavlovna, Elena, 96
Pavlovsk, Residency of, **129-134**
Perugino, 105
Peter I the Great, 8, 9c, 10c, 20, 20c, 22, 23c, 24, 24c, 25c, 27c, 30, 35, 49, 49c, 50, 51c, 52, 52c, 55, 56, 56c, 59, 60, 60c, 61, 62, 65, 69, 73c, 75, 77, 80c, 89, 102, 102c, 103c, 105, 108, 110, 113c, 114, 120, 120c, 126c
Peterhof, Palace of, 13c, 27, 27c, 30, 30c, 46c, **108-119**
Peter II, 24, 25c, 105
Peter III, 29
Peter-Paul Cathedral, 10, 33c, 35c, 38c, **50-59**
Petipa, Marius, 94, 94c
Petrograd, 42, 43c, 44, 44c, 45, 50c
Petrogradskaya (Petrograd Island), 8c, 10c, 36
Picasso, Pablo, 82, 87c
Pil Tower, 129
Pimenov, Nikolai, 96
Pimenov, Stepan, 61c, 67, 122c
Pineau, Nicolas, 113c
Piskarevskoye Cemetery, 48c, 105c
Poland, 20, 33c
Polenov, Vasily, 98
Pollux, 61
Poltava, battle of, 20, 20c, 22, 23c, 114
Popkov, 46, 48
Port-Arthur, 41c
Porto, A., 55c
Potemkin, battleship, 41, 43c
Potemkin, Prince, 76, 100, 107, 107c, 113c
Prokofiev, Ivan, 93
Pulkovo, 47
Pushkin, Alexander, 12, 35c, 60, 89, 89c, 90, 90c, 96, 96c, 122c, 126
Putilov, factory, 41, 44, 44c

Q
Quarenghi, Giacomo, 10c, 30, 30c, 56, 56c, 59, 61, 69c, 73, 73c, 76, 77c, 100, 105, 106, 107c, 126, 131

R
Radiscev, Alexander, 50
Raphaello, 73, 73c, 75, 133
Rasputin, Grigory, 42, 43c, 90
Rastrelli, Bartolomeo Carlo, 103c
Rastrelli, Bartolomeo Francesco, 3, 27, 27c, 29, 46c, 67, 69, 70, 70c, 90, 102, 102c, 120, 120c, 106, 108c, 110, 113c, 114c, 122c, 123, 125c, 126c
Razumovsky, Alexei, 100
Red Square, 69
Reed, John, 65
Rembrandt, 70, 82
Reni, Guido, 105
Renoir, Pierre Auguste, 82, 84c
Repin, Ilya, 99
Resurrection, Cathedral of the, 3c
Rezanov, A., 38
Rinaldi, Antonio, 30, 55, 126
Romanov dynasty, 38c, 40, 50, 52, 125
Rome, 8, 62c, 76c, 90, 93c, 107
Ropscin hills, 114

Rossi Street, 100c, 101c
Rossi, Carlo, 10, 10c, 35, 61, 67, 67c, 75, 96, 100, 100c, 105, 131
Rotari, Pietro Antonio, 27c, 113, 113c
Rubens, 82, 105
Rubinstein, Arthur, 96
Rublev, Andrei, 98
Russia, 8, 10, 20, 20c, 21, 22, 29, 29c, 32c, 33, 35, 35c, 36, 38, 40, 43c, 45, 49, 49c, 50, 59c, 61, 65, 67, 69c, 93, 94c, 96, 107c, 114, 114c, 122c, 124c, 125, 126, 131
Russian Museum, 27c, 96, 96c, 98, 99c
Rustciuk, 38c

S
Sadovaya Street, 100
Saltykov-Schedrin, Library, 100
Saliapin, Fedor, 90c
Samson, 114
Samsonev, Alexei, 20c
Sardinia, King of, 105c
Sardinia, Kingdom of, 36, 36c
Satire, Theater of, 100
Schaedel, Gottfried, 59
Schedrin, 61c
Schilder, 36c
Schinkel, Karl, 102
Schlusselburg Fort, 46
Schluter, Andreas, 123
School of Naval Engineering, 60c
Scukin S., 75, 87c
Scythians, 78, 81c
Senate Square, 9c, 46, 46c
Serangeli, Gioacchin-Giuseppe, 32c
Seremetiev Palace, 102, 102c
Shenkel, K. F., 10c
Shostakovitch, Dimitry, 47
Siberia, 36c, 56, 126
Simon Magus, 50
Slavianka, 129, 129c
Slisselburg, 55
Small Winter Canal, 12c, 73
Smolny Convent, 3, 10, 27, 27c, 30, **89-107**
Smolny Institute, 30, 44, 45
Sobcak, Anatoly, 49
Solokha Comb, 13c
Soviet Union, 45, 47, 106
St. Basil's Cathedral, 38
St. Isaac's Cathedral, 9c, 12c, 46c, 60, 62, 62c
St. Isaac's Square, 35, 36, 65, 65c
St. Lazarus' graveyard, 105
St. Paul's Cathedral (London), 62c
St. Peter's Basilica (Rome), 62c, 93, 93c
St. Petersburg Conservatory, 35c
St. Petersburg History Museum, 55
St. Petersburg Philharmonica, 96
Stakenschneider, Andrei, 10c, 36, 55, 65, 65c, 76, 76c, 104c
Stalin, 45, 45c
Starov, Ivan, 105, 107, 107c
Stasov, Vasily, 3c, 35, 70c, 73, 73c, 74c, 105, 106, 125, 126
Stasov, Vladimir, 35c
Stolypin, Petr, 41
Strelka, 56, 56c
Stroganov Palace, 90, 98
Suvarov, Alexander, Marshal, 100, 105, 105c
Swans' Canal, 102
Sweden, 20, 114
Swedes, 10c, 22, 50

T
Tatiana, Grand Duchess, 42c
Tatlin, 99c
Tauride Palace, 107, 107c
Tchaikovsky, 105
Terebenev, Ivan, 60, 61c, 69c, 73
Thebes, 59, 59c
Tichvin Cemetery, 10c
Tichvin, 46, 47
Tilsit, 32c
Tobolsk, 45c
Ton, Konstantin, 36c
Trezzini, Domenico, 21, 27c, 50, 52, 52c, 59, 69, 102, 104c, 105
Trinity Bridge, 10c, 50c
Tropinin, Vasily, 98
Trotsky, Leon, 44c
Tsushima Island, 40
Turkey, 36, 36c
Turks, 107c, 113
Tuvolkov, 113

U
Ukraine, 79c
Ulyanov, Alexander, 50
United States, 48c
University, 57c
Upper Bavaria, 99c
Ural mountains, 62, 71c, 73c, 76, 125c, 132c
Usakov, Simon, 98

V
Vallin de la Mothe, Jean-Baptiste, 30, 59, 65, 70, 90, 100, 113
Van Dyck, 73c, 105
Van Gogh, Vincent, 82, 84c, 99c
Vasilevsky Island, 22, 48c, **50-59**
Vatican Museums, 73, 73c
Velten, Georg, 30
Venecianov, Alexei, 98
Venice, 8, 20c
Viardot, Pauline, 90c
Victoria, Queen, 41c
Victory Square, 8c, 48
Vitali, Ivan, 62, 129c
Vitebsk, 98c
Volchov, 56
Volga, 56
Voltaire, 29
Voronikhin, Andrei, 35, 90, 90c, 93, 93c, 105, 131, 132c

W
Winter Canal, 12c, 35c, 73
Winter Palace, 8c, 10, 13c, 27, 27c, 29, 33, 40, 44c, 45, 45c, 55, 67, 67c, 68, **69-87**, 100
Wren, Christopher, 22

Y
Yaroslavitch, Alexander, 23c
Yusupov, Felix, 90
Yusupov Palace, 90, 90c
Yusupov, Princes, 75, 90

Z
Zacharov, Andrian, 60, 60c, 105
Zayachy Island (Hare Island), 50
Zdanov, 45, 46
Zemcov, 120c
Zinovyev, 45

136 As blue as the sky and splendid as the sun, pure gold covering its five domes, the royal chapel in Czarskoye Selo dates from 1740. Designed by K.I. Tchevakinsky, it stands at the northeast end of the sumptuous facade of the 984 foot long palace. The St. Petersburg imperial residences were built to satisfy the whims of the czars and to equal the magnificence of European palaces, in particular, Versailles. Thanks to the combined efforts of brilliant architects and an abundant workforce, they may even have exceeded the beauty of the French palace.